Ask Papa Jack

Ask Papa Jack

**Wisdom of the
World's Oldest CEO**

STEVEN E. WEIL

JOHNSON BOOKS
BOULDER

Copyright © 2009 by Steven E. Weil

All rights reserved.
No part of this publication may be reproduced or transmitted
in any form or by any means, electronic or mechanical,
including photocopy, recording, or any information storage and retrieval system,
without permission in writing from the publisher.

Published by Johnson Books,
a Big Earth Publishing company.
1637 Pearl Street, Suite 201, Boulder, Colorado 80302.
1-800-258-5830
E-mail: books@bigearthpublishing.com
www.bigearthpublishing.com

Cover and text design by Rebecca Finkel
cover photo by Rick Wilking/Reuters

9 8 7 6 5 4 3 2 1

Library of Congress Cataloging-in-Publication Data
Weil, Steven E.
Ask Papa Jack: wisdom from the world's oldest CEO / Steven E. Weil.
p. cm.
Includes bibliographical references and index.
ISBN 978-1-55566-428-2 (alk. paper)
1. Chief executive officers—West (U.S.)
2. Anecdotes—West (U.S.)
3. Shirt's, Men's—West (U.S.) I. Title.
HD38.25.U6W45 2009
338.7'687115092—dc22
2008053536

Printed in the United States of America

In Memoriam

Papa Jack

March 28, 1901—August 13, 2008

107 Years Young

Author's Note

The manuscript for this book went to the publisher prior to Papa Jack's death. While it was my hope he would enjoy it, it was not to be. This is but one tribute to an extraordinary man who lived an extraordinary life.

We were overwhelmed by the media response of his death. His story was syndicated and appeared locally, nationally, and internationally in hundreds of newspapers, in addition to *The New Yort Times,* National Public Radio, *CBS Sunday Morning,* and *The Economist.*

Why speak of him in the past when his impact very much remains in the present and future?

❖ ❖ ❖

Contents

Preface xi
Acknowledgments xv

Introduction 1
Chronology 5

CHAPTER 1
On Being "Papa Jack" 15

CHAPTER 2
History, Stories, and Words to Live By 21

CHAPTER 3
Papa Jack's Unique Sense of Humor 33

CHAPTER 4
On Romance 37

CHAPTER 5
On Integrity and Values 45

CHAPTER 6
On Business 51

CHAPTER 7
On the Western Business 77

CHAPTER 8
On Driving 85

CHAPTER 9
On Life 93

CHAPTER 10
On Longevity 99

CHAPTER 11
Postscript: "It'll go forever if you just play it right" ... 109

◆ ◆ ◆

Dedication

This book is dedicated to my Dad,
Jack B. Weil (1928–2008).

MY BOOK *Western Shirts: A Classic American Fashion,* was dedicated to Papa Jack, but this one is about him. We never expected our grandfather to outlive his son—my father—who died in 2008. We all thought Dad would live into old age like his father and grandfather.

Dad was part of our limelight but in its shadow. He did not start the company, but he was vital to its later success. He called himself the "meatball" sandwiched between Papa and I, the bread. He was never president, the post occupied by his father for over sixty years. Moreover, as he once pointed out in a TV interview, how could he retire when his father would not?

Dad was a creative force at Rockmount for fifty years. He was passionate about color, texture, composition, fabric, and design details. He modernized his father's business and maintained it for the next generation. He laid the foundation of our signature designs and let me build upon it.

He was generous to a fault, a model for the rest of us. At an age when others retire, we mortgaged our houses to buy the Rockmount building from the family. He knew firsthand the many shortcomings typical of family businesses, and he did not perpetuate them. He insured an orderly succession of the company, the lack of which has led to the demise of many family businesses.

He was a devoted son and father. He worked with his father for over fifty years and his son for over twenty-five. He ate lunch daily with his father for most of their careers. When I began running the company, I asked him to weigh in on important decisions. I miss being able to ask him those questions, but I know that he instilled in me a sense of the right course of action. I hope to do him justice.

—STEVEN E. WEIL

❖ ❖ ❖

Preface

"There was never an uninteresting life.
Such a thing is an impossibility."
—MARK TWAIN

THE INSPIRATION for this book is my grandfather, Papa Jack. As the family patriarch, he was always important to those related to him, but as the market he created grew, his profile emerged globally. It is really amazing how the arcane fashion idea of snap shirts became an American fashion icon worn around the world.

Back in the 1930s and '40s, his reach was regional. In the 1950s and '60s, it became national in scope. Finally, after three generations, it is international. When we introduced retail in 2000, the Rockmount flagship store became a destination, drawing visitors from across the globe.

While I read the press releases as they hit over the years, I never reviewed the body in its entirety until researching this book. Papa's notoriety overwhelmed me as I went year-by-year reading press coverage that was first local, then national, and finally global. The bottom line is that Papa Jack started and popularized a lifestyle. Moreover, he did it with integrity and kindness.

Parts of this book came from the archives that we began maintaining when I joined the company in 1981. I sensed, even as a youngster, something important and historical about my grandfather and the company he started. As an adult, it seemed natural to preserve pieces of the mosaic. Admittedly it is difficult, if not impossible, to do justice in reducing a lifetime spanning over one hundred years to these pages. How to express his intense warmth, great depth of personality, and rich humor?

His worldview came from another time, yet remained profoundly relevant. He scoffed at modern ideas most of us accept, such as impersonal company answering machines; bigger is better; debt leverage; and corporate images created by focus groups. He never used the term "entrepreneur," but its definition could feature his picture. He knew of celebrities who wore Rockmount over the years, such as Elvis and Robert Redford, but later ones like David Bowie, Bob Dylan, and Eric Clapton were not on his playlist.

I returned to Colorado in 1981 to work in the family business after graduate school for a Master's degree in law and politics in England. Papa Jack, at age eighty-one, was president. My father, Jack B., was about the age I am now and served as vice president. Combined, they had over nine decades of practical business experience. Neither had taken a business course, yet both were intensely entrepreneurial—Papa Jack started the business, he and my father and built it.

I decided to get a Master's degree in Business Administration while working for the company full-time so I could take over when needed. Who could know that Papa Jack would remain president and Jack B. vice president for another twenty-five years? For many years we joked that Papa was waiting for my dad and me to retire so he could take over.

Papa took delight in the world every day, be it with his family, his company, his customers, or anyone he happened to meet. His approach was never cliché. His personality was one of a kind: penetrating mind, photographic memory, mathematically astute, deeply curious. This is my grandfather's life story, as best as it can be put into words. He believed in the power of stories and told them prolifically. It is fitting to tell his story through the sum of these many anecdotes, stories, and "Papa-isms."

◆ ◆ ◆

Acknowledgments

IF FAMILY BUSINESSES were easy to run, more would survive. My grandfather was a visionary who started a business that he and my father passionately built, and later, enabled me to carry on. They devoted their lives to running the family business—this story would be very different otherwise.

The Denver community supported our business when it reinvented itself in recent years. Had that not happened, we might be just another family business casualty.

The State of Colorado Historic Perservation Fund awarded us a grant to help enable the restoration of the one-hundred-year-old Rockmount building for the next hundred years. The Prairie Style building that my grandfather chose simply as a suitable warehouse was later viewed by my father and me as integral to our identity. Its renovation gave us new life, enabling us to remain in our historic home, now the last of our species at the site where Denver had its beginnings in 1858.

The media coverage of Rockmount has spread worldwide. While the substance of this book is stories that Papa Jack repeated countless times over the years, the media has contributed to an archive for posterity. Print, radio, and television are quoted in much of this work.

I thank my wife, Wendy, and son, Colter, for letting my work intrude on our family time. My laptop, open at swim meets, on driving trips, and in the family room, seems to be another member of the family …

I should also thank that Tulane English professor who, long ago, mercilessly ripped apart a freshman honors English essay and started me on the road to better writing. There are also those who, over the years, allowed me to work on yearbooks, school newspapers, catalogs, and real newspaper editorials, which helped, too. Also, Gibbs Smith believed in my story and published the *Western Shirt* book, which led to this one.

Finally, I would like to thank two people for their roles behind the scenes: my agent Nancy Stauffer who brought me to Johnson Books, and my publisher Mira Perrizo who gave the book its finished shape.

❖ ❖ ❖

Introduction

ARE WE WRONG to idolize others? My grandfather has always been my hero. He was the family patriarch nearly forever, yet he was young at heart. More than charismatic, he was an emotional bedrock, a leader. Deep down he was just like the rest of us, only better. He did far more than live a long life—he lived it well. He started a family, became its head for four generations. He founded a business, became its head for sixty years. He started a fashion, but that is different, for you can't *run* a fashion or an industry. You can't herd cats or good ideas. This was viral marketing without the net, at a personal level—just as Papa Jack would have it. The virus germinated the hard way, reaching one person at a time, over many years, then exploded. What started in the West has now reached across the globe, both in popularity and sourcing.

On a personal level, Papa Jack taught me so much: integrity, a solid outlook on life, a strong work ethic, how to run a business and add to its value, how to find joy in small things. His legacy is a quality that is hard to reduce to words. A good life is a work of art. In Spock's words, *live long and prosper.*

What kind of person was Papa Jack? He took delight in so much, and nothing made his eyes light up like kids and dogs. He reached each and every person in a special way. Whether by giving a five year old a broken pocket watch to take apart, taking a college student out for a ride to talk, kneeling down to make a three year old laugh, or greeting the mailman, he touched us all. In his later years, so many people came to think of him as a surrogate grandfather, perhaps a universal grandfather.

Papa Jack was rarely ill. He was only in the hospital a couple times in the last fifty years; people seem to live shorter lives there, so it's a good place to avoid if you want to live longer. The last time he was hospitalized was in the early 1990s for an angioplasty to open a clogged artery. Our mailman surprised us when he dropped by the hospital to visit. Does your mailman come to see you when you're ill? Papa Jack cast a spell on everyone he touched. His reach once only extended to those he met in person, by phone, or by mail. Later he drew the media's attention, and his impact spread.

While I was researching this book, my friend Andrew Hudson told me, "I never had a grandfather that I knew." (Andrew helped arrange the first Denver street sign change in 2001, in which Wazee Street was temporarily renamed

"Jack A. Weil Boulevard.") This made me realize how lucky I was to have had a grandfather all my life, all the more so for having worked with him over twenty-seven years.

He reminded so many people of their own grandfathers. He was an archetype, like George, the one-hundred-year-old land tortoise in the Galapagos who is the last of his kind. This is Papa Jack's story, in his own words and the words of those who knew him. They are words of wisdom to live by.

❖ ❖ ❖

Chronology

JACK A. WEIL

MARCH 28, 1901
Jack A. Weil is born in Evansville, Indiana, to Sarah and Abraham Weil.

1909
Jack delivers milk to the needy using a wagon pulled by a goat.

1912
Jack is one of the first Boy Scouts in America when the organization first came to the U.S. from the U.K.

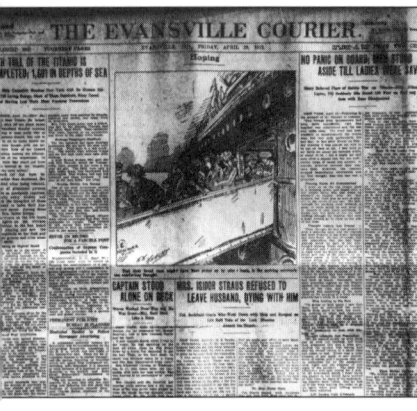

1914

Jack begins his first job, delivering newspapers six days a week with brother Edgar in a horse and buggy for *Evansville Press* (which later became *Press Courier*), a Scripps Howard publication. They make half a cent on each one-cent paper sold and have over one hundred customers. When they graduate from high school, each has saved one thousand dollars. Later, still a youngster, Jack is promoted to distributor for other paper boys. (Courtesy Mizell Stewart III, Editor, *Evansville Courier & Press*)

1917

Jack and Edgar buy their first car, a Model "T" Ford.

Sunday School photo 1917 (Jack at far right)

1918

During World War I, Jack works after school at D.S. Bernstein Overall Factory and learns apparel manufacturing.

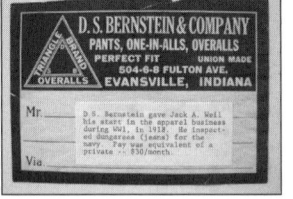

Jack graduates from high school. He starts the Evansville Sales Service, a dry good wholesaler, with friend Bill Drucker.

1926

A. Stein & Company, Jack's employer at the time, transfers him to the South. He buys a new Chrysler Roadster, serial number 33. This is the car he drives to Colorado. He would drive Chryslers for the next seventy-five years.

June 22 Jack marries Beatrice "Bea" Baum in Humboldt, Tennessee.

1928

January Jack and Bea move to Denver, first living at the Cosmopolitan Hotel, then an apartment at Park Avenue and Humboldt Street. Later they move to the brand new Park Lane Hotel on Washington Park. Jack opens an office for A. Stein & Co. to market Paris Garters. "When I came to Denver, Highway 40 down Colfax was a gravel road," he recalled.

November 13
Beatrice gives birth to their first child, Jack B.

Employees of A. Stein & Co. (Jack at bottom left)

1935

During the Depression, Jack goes into the Western business with partner Phil Miller in the Stockman Supply, originally a wholesale jobber of jeans and hats sold to farmers and working cowboys. Jack persuades chambers of commerce and rodeo officials to promote their towns and events by wearing Western clothing. The strategy works, and the firm, now called Miller & Co., prospers.

November 19
Beatrice gives birth to their daughter, Jane (Weil Romberg).

Seven-year-old Jack B.

World War II:
Jack serves as an air raid warden in Denver.

1939

Jack buys their first home at 233 Belaire Street. He saved for eleven years to pay for it in cash because he did not believe in debt or living beyond his means.

1946
Founds the Town Club social club and Rose Hospital. Becomes board member for Temple Emanuel.

Founds Rockmount Ranch Wear Manufacturing Co., 1626 Wazee Street. His signature shirt design with sawtooth pockets and diamond snaps will become the longest-running shirt design in the U.S.

1954

Son, Jack B. Weil, joins Rockmount. Bea urges him to join the firm, saying, "Your father is not getting any younger. Come home and try this for a year." Jack B. expands the company's market nationally, and later takes over design and merchandising, which he runs for over thirty-five years. He works at the firm for fifty-four years.

LATE 1950s
Founds Temple Micah.

1959
First photo of three generations appears in print. Who could imagine that this will lead to the three of them working together much of their careers?

Third generation Steven with his grandfather Jack A. Weil, and be-whiskered dad Jack B. Weil; the beard is temporary in honor of Colorado's Centennial. Young Steven, 18 months, is already a model and "showpiece" in his western outfit. This picture was taken in the sample room of the Rockmount Ranch Wear business office at 1636 Lawrence St. in Denver, Colorado.

1960s
Papa Jack introduces computers to Rockmount.

1981
June 21 Grandson Steve Weil joins Rockmount after receiving degrees from Tulane University and the University of Bristol, England. While working full-time he completes an MBA at University of Colorado (1985). Steve handles advertising and extends Rockmount's market internationally, and eventually takes over design and merchandising.

1986
Papa Jack receives Industry Pioneer Award at the Denver Western Market Trade Show.

1990
June 23 Papa Jack's wife, Bea, dies at age eighty-nine, after sixty-four years of marriage.

EARLY 1990s
Papa Jack is hospitalized for an angioplasty—his first hospital visit in decades—and returns promptly to work.

1993
April 18 Papa Jack is recognized by *The New York Times* for making the first shirts with snaps.

1995
Papa Jack receives Industry Lifetime Achievement Award at Dallas Western Market Trade Show.

1997
Papa Jack receives Industry Service Award at Denver Western Market Trade Show.

1999
Papa Jack learns Windows computer operating system.

2001

January Wazee Street is honorarily renamed by Denver's Mayor Webb "Jack A. Weil Way" in recognition of Papa Jack's 100th birthday. This tradition continues each year.

April 1
First worldwide syndicated news story, by Colleen Long of Associated Press, appears in the *Los Angeles Times*: "Rockmount Ranch Wear Ropes in Clients by Bucking Retail Trendiness."

May 10
Weil family and Rockmount receive their first worldwide television coverage on a CNN feature by Gina London.

2003

April 25 Associated Press runs a worldwide syndicated news story "Venerable Western Clothier Bucks Trends," by Catherine Tsai.

2005

May Eric Clapton wears a Rockmount shirt at the Cream Reunion Concert, Royal Albert Hall, London.

The Times (London) interview is published, in which Papa Jack calls Wal-Mart "sons of bitches" and Sam Walton a "hillbilly."

December
Steve Weil's book, *Western Shirts: A Classic American Fashion*, is published, and dedicated to Papa Jack.

Jack A., Jack B., and Steve receive Historic Denver Preservation Award.

November
Historic renovation of Rockmount building is completed. Flagship retail store and museum opens at 1626 Wazee.

2006

February Rockmount shirts that were worn in the movie *Brokeback Mountain* sell for $101,000 on eBay.

CBS Evening News features Rockmount and the Weils.

Jack A., Jack B., and Steve receive the Downtown Denver Partnership Award.

Jack A., Jack B., and Steve receive the Fashion Group International Forum Award.

March Rockmount is a feature on fashion in *The New York Times*.

The New York Times runs the story on Heath Ledger and Jake Gyllenhaal, who wore Rockmount shirts in the movie *Brokeback Mountain*.

2007

March Steve is appointed president of Rockmount

April 27 NPR's *Morning Edition* has a feature story on Rockmount and Papa Jack's 106th birthday

June A national advertising campaign for the city of Denver features "Ask for Papa Jack" billboards in major cities.

Fodor's Travel Guide features Rockmount as "One of the last real Western landmarks."

True West Magazine names Rockmount "Best Designer."

2007 *(continued)*

July, 20 Bob Dylan shops at Rockmount flagship store in Denver and spends $1,200. He knows his way around, as he's shopped here before.

October 7 CBS *60 Minutes'* has a Bruce Springsteen interview with Scott Pelley, who is wearing a Rockmount denim shirt.

November Jack A., Jack B., and Steve receive the tourism Star Award from Denver Metro Convention and Visitor Bureau. This is Jack B.'s last public appearance.

November 15–December 26 AOL.com, MSN.com, and Inc.com features worldwide home page that is titled "The Centenarian Cowboy," on Papa Jack and Rockmount.

December 5 CNBC runs an interview with Papa Jack.

December Employees at Rockmount know the Democratic National Convention is coming to Denver before official announcement because of the shirt order placed by the central committee.

2008

January 23 Papa Jack's son, Jack B. Weil, dies at the age of 79.

March 12 Rockmount and Weil family receive the Limelight Award, LoDo Historic District.

May 28 Curious Theater performs play "107 Short Plays About Papa Jack Weil," part of the "Denver Stories" series. This is Papa Jack's last public celebration, although he continues to work every day.

August 10 *The New York Times* article by Eric Wilson, "36 Hours in Denver for the DNC" features Rockmount in the Top 10 things to do in Denver during the Democratic National Convention.

2008 *(continued)*
August 13 Papa Jack Weil dies at the age of 107.

August 14 *The New York Times* runs a story "Jack A. Weil, the Cowboy's Dresser, Dies at 107," by Douglas Martin.

August 14 The *Rocky Mountain News* runs a front-page story, "Oldest working CEO Jack Weil dies at 107," by John Ensslin.

August 17 *CBS Sunday Morning* airs a feature on the life of Papa Jack.

August 18 The *Rocky Mountain News* runs a front-page story and photo, "Memorial held for Jack A. Weil 'the universal grandpa': Hundreds honor man whose business was symbol of West," by John Ensslin.

August 19 *The Washington Post* runs the article "Jack A. Weil: Entrepreneur Put Style in Western Wear," by Martin Weil.

August 19 The *Los Angeles Times* runs an Associated Press worldwide syndicated story, "Jack A. Weil, 107: designed, popularized cowboy shirts with snap fasteners," by Barry Gutierrez.

August 28 *The Economist* runs the article "Jack A. Weil, patriarch of western clothing, died August 13th, aged 107."

August 15 *The Denver Post* runs an editorial page cartoon, "Papa Jack Weil 1901–2008," by Mike Keefe.

August 15 National Public Radio/ *All Things Considered* airs "Oldest CEO and Popularizer of Cowboy Shirts Dies: Jack Weil's grandson Steven Weil discusses the man who died Wednesday and the successful business."

August 15 The *Chicago Tribune* runs an Associated Press worldwide syndicated story and photo, "Jack A. Weil, 1901–2008, Maker of iconic cowboy wear, Denver company's snap-buttoned Western shirts have longtime following among entertainers," by Ivan Moreno.

CHAPTER 1

On Being "Papa Jack"

HE WAS "PAPA" for an entire generation—over forty years. At the age of three, my son Colter renamed him "Papa Jack." The name stuck. If you google "Papa Jack" he comes up. How many people in the world can you google their nickname?

Papa Jack's mental acuity was amazing. We think he had a photographic memory. He remembered the most minute details. He knew the layout of streets in small towns he had not visited in fifty years. Just before his death, we drove past a church on Seventeenth Street, and Papa commented that it was the church where his grandson Greg married Laurie Romberg. The wedding was in 1987, the first and last time either of us had been to that church. I had forgotten, but he had not.

Papa Jack possessed the ability to do complex math in his head. When I began taking over the factory management from him in the late 1980s, I set up pricing models on the computer to update changing overhead, labor, and raw materials costs. This was when Lotus spreadsheets first came out. Papa Jack reviewed the numbers with me, doing all the math in his head. I often raced him, first with a calculator

and later with a spreadsheet. He would invariably finish various algebraic formulas about the same time I did, and always laughed when I confirmed him correct.

Today I maintain hundreds of spreadsheets on our finances and product costs. Papa ran the company for decades with what he called the "computer in my head."

◈ The Man With the Answers

Did Papa Jack actually process information differently than the rest of us? He grew up in the abacus era, long before electronic calculators. He ran complex calculations in his head, and he ran them fast. For that matter, he retained most of the company administration in his head. It was easier to find that way—his desk was piled deep with papers. A motto in his office said: "a clean desk is the sign of a sick mind." We went to him for answers.

Who better to ask advice of?

◈ Mechanical Aptitude

Papa Jack had a great mechanical aptitude. Many years ago I asked him what career he might have chosen if things were different. He answered "civil engineering." That makes sense on a lot of levels. He was fascinated by construction projects. Whenever we passed a street project, he would wonder aloud about what they were doing. When a building was being built downtown, he commented that they tear down better buildings in New York than we build in Denver.

Papa Jack was deeply involved in the technical aspects of running our Ft. Smith, Arkansas, shirt factory for fifty years. He knew every piece of machinery and purchased customized automated equipment as needed. Some of that machinery remains in production today, decades later.

In the 1940s, Papa Jack designed a smile pocket shirt. He wanted embroidered arrows on the ends of the pockets, so he took a machine that embroidered stars and had it converted to sew only one point of the star, thus forming the arrow shape he wanted. That machine operated for decades.

> "He is a pragmatist in the extreme . . . There is nobody better I can go to for answers to the hard questions. He brings integrity and consistent ethics that are sadly lacking elsewhere."
>
> —Steve Weil, *St. Petersburg Times*, "Famous Before the Movie," March 28, 2006

◆ Can You Ever Have Too Much Experience?

Papa Jack's life experience spanned over a century. When he was born in 1901, William McKinley was president. Electricity and indoor plumbing were novelties. His first transportation was a goat cart. He later got around by horse and buggy, and eventually drove a long line of cars tracing the evolution of the automobile. Papa Jack started in business before calculators existed, and ended up using Windows everyday.

There are many types of experience. Some people do what they do for decades, merely repeating what they learned the first year every year after. Papa Jack was extraordinary in his ability to draw on his life experiences to solve problems creatively. Many challenges he had seen before and easily recalled a successful solution. New problems required new solutions, but they just took a little longer to address. He was remarkable for many things. He retained complex details and vivid memories from a vast lifetime of experiences.

◆ Government Efficiency

Papa Jack was a political conservative with a sense of humor, a lifelong Republican, a proponent of limited government and a balanced budget. He was the ultimate private sector guy, devoted to an individual's right, power, and responsibility to control his own destiny, free of government nuisance.

This wood carving marked "Government Surplus" sat in a place of honor near Papa Jack's desk, expressing his faith in the potential of government efficiency. A friend made it for him over fifty years ago. It pokes fun at government waste.

◈ Say It Straight

Papa Jack was a populist, and that was a lot of his charm. He was as comfortable with company presidents as warehouse employees, and treated both with respect. An old friend of his, Mac Baldridge, secretary of commerce under Reagan, put the president in touch with Papa Jack. Papa took offense to Reagan's public statement that the United States was transitioning from a manufacturing base to a service economy. In response, he wrote a homespun parable to Reagan: "You come from Dixon, Illinois, not far from my hometown of Evansville, Indiana. Where we come from 'servicing' is when you take the mare to the stud." Reagan wrote back "Jack, Washington is a long way from Dixon, Illinois." He liked to tell this story often.

◈ On Lunch

Over the years Papa and Dad ate lunch together most days. When I started working at Rockmount in the 1980s, I would often join them. We ate lunch at a different place every day. Sometimes we would get in the car and have no idea where we were going until we got there. Papa drove and took delight in surprising us. It was fun because he knew varied and obscure places. In the last twenty years that changed. Papa and Dad began to eat at the Denver Athletic Club, and they were regular fixtures at the same table almost every day. Papa said, "I like going where they know me."

◈ Why Buy Back Old Rockmount Shirts?

Papa Jack was not a collector in the sense of surrounding himself with art and things. No, he was practical and kept only what he could use. Back in the early 1980s, I was browsing through a Los Angeles vintage store on Melrose Avenue, and found an embroidered brown gabardine shirt that was so old I didn't at first recognize it as Rockmount. It dated from the 1940s and was marked $75, which was twice the price of Rockmount shirts then. I told the retailer it was one of the first Western shirts my grandfather had made.

Touched, he told me to take the shirt and send him a couple of new ones for it. Excited by the find, I didn't wait until returning home to tell my grandfather. In those pre-cell phone days I found a phone booth and called the office. "WHAT?" Papa exclaimed, "You traded two perfectly good new shirts for an old one we sold for $3 forty years ago?"

CHAPTER 2

History, Stories, and Words to Live By

WE LIVE BY STORIES. We learn from stories in a way far more deeply than any other way short of actual experience. If you grew up before television, as humans did for millennia up until the last five minutes of human history, telling stories was the way you transmitted history, culture, knowledge, values, religion, and all else that mattered. In an era when storytelling is becoming a vanishing art, Papa Jack continued the great tradition of Mark Twain past and Garrison Keillor present. He not only brought history alive, he was history.

His countless stories are still like unforgettable movies in the collective mind of my family. His photographic memory for detail made them come alive. Often, he ended them with a mischievous grin.

THE CANOE

Grandson Greg Romberg asked Papa to retell this story for the book.

We ordered a canoe kit by mail when I was fourteen years old. We built it in the basement. We measured the size of the window it would go through, but did not take into consideration the neighbor's fence with roses growing on it across the walkway.

We found out we needed more room to go through the window. First I went down to the neighbor, a banker, Mr. Enlow, who said, "Don't you touch my wire fence and climbing roses."

So we got up at five in the morning and took the fence down. We took the canoe out. So far as Mr. Enlow is concerned, the canoe is still in the basement.

We took it up to the waterworks. The Ohio River was a mile wide. We had one paddle. I had to be the first one to paddle it down the river. I got caught in the current and couldn't get it to shore. About two miles down the river there was a bend where I finally got it to the bank. Well, the fire department was there—the police department, too. I got out but the canoe went down the river.

◆ His Father's Story

Abraham Weil, Papa Jack's father, immigrated to the United States in 1871, when he was fifteen years old. He fled his native town of Mulhouse, located in what was then Alsace Lorraine, during the Franco-Prussian War. When the Prussians invaded, they inducted young boys to march in front of their army as human shields. The French would not fire on their own youth.

Rather than being pressed into the enemy army, young Abe boarded a train in Alsace, on the Franco-Prussian border, and headed for the port city of Calais, on the French coast. Along the way, the Prussians stopped the train, locked the side facing the French border, and ordered everyone off on the Prussian side. Abe used his pocketknife to jimmy the lock on the French side of the train and escaped, leaving his possessions on board.

The Prussians on the other side demanded he come over to them. The French soldiers told them, "Come get him." He then continued on his journey to the coast.

Abe made his way to the United States aboard a ship, and the trip took four weeks. Abe left France at the same time as the French impressionists, including Monet, Pissarro, Tissot, and others, were fleeing. I often daydream that Abe met them on the journey and we will someday find an odd napkin sketched with his portrait! On arrival in the states, Abe traveled to Mount Vernon, Indiana, where there was a small German-Jewish community. They asked him,

"What can you do?" The community had no rabbi, and Abe had studied Judaism, so he taught religion to the children.

Abe was open-minded and had a liberal view of religion. He was a Reform Jew, a branch emerging at the time of the French Revolution. This modern movement maintained a delicate balance between allegiance to nationality and religious beliefs. It spread to America largely by German immigrants during the mid–1800s, becoming the dominant branch of Judaism. Abe also understood the more conservative practices and led services for Orthodox Russian Jews as well.

True to his liberal views, Abe did not keep kosher. Papa Jack recalled that when he was a child, a rabbi came to his father and said, "Abe, you are a leader here. What am I to say when people ask how come you do not keep kosher?"

Abe responded, "It's more important what comes out of your mouth than what goes in it." Later, as he and his dad walked away, Abe said, "What would they think if they knew Jesus said that?"

◆ Early Telephones

I asked Papa when his parents got their first telephone. He said they always had one. "The phones were not very good then," he said, "and you had to speak loudly." When Papa's father Abe was on the phone long distance, his wife Sarah would tell him, "Why don't you open the windows, they could hear you better."

I remember that Papa always spoke loudly on long distance calls. Some habits never die . . .

◈ Papa Jack's First Business

After graduating from high school, Papa and his friend Bill Drucker started Evansville Sales Service, a dry goods wholesale jobber. They sold name-brand clothing to independently owned stores.

They were in business until a coal strike in southern Illinois culminated with the unions burning down the town, and the stores they sold to were all ruined. Papa and Fred lost their investment. They called their supplier, A. Stein & Company of Chicago, to whom they owed money. The treasurer came down to see them about the debt. He recommended bankruptcy. Papa replied, "Age nineteen is too young to go bankrupt. I never bought anything I did not pay for." He repaid his half of the debt by

going to work as a salesman for A. Stein & Company. He was the youngest salesman ever hired by the company.

Typically, salesmen traveled by train. He convinced the sales manager to allow him to use an automobile. He was the first at the company to get one, an Essex four-cylinder Hudson. By the end of the year, every A. Stein & Co. salesman—there were over thirty—had a car.

◆ Go West, Young Man

When Papa was asked how he came to Denver, he would answer, "My firm gave me the area between the Mexican border and the Canadian border, but the total population was less than Cook County." His firm, A. Stein & Company, which sold Paris Garters, sent him to Denver to open a sales office there.

> *"I came to Denver in 1928. It was a wonderful place for a young man to come. There was every opportunity in the world."*
> —9 News KUSA, December 9, 2004

Papa related that as he was driving on Highway 40 across the plains in a new 1926 Chrysler Roadster, "I saw the afternoon sun shining on the Rocky Mountains and turned to my wife and said, 'This is it.'

"Denver was a great city, about 200,000 people. There were cops on the corners directing traffic." (*Rocky Mountain News*, January 11, 2001)

DON'T LEAVE YOUR GLASSES ON WHEN YOU STICK YOUR HEAD OUT THE AIRPLANE WINDOW

When I was with A. Stein & Company in the late '20s, we lived in the Park Lane Hotel in Denver. I was in Montana on business. I rode in a plane that was establishing a mail and passenger route. They had to fly a certain number of passenger hours before getting a permit.

The pilot sat next to me at breakfast while I was in Billings, Montana, on business. He offered me a ride to Denver. I had been on the train, which takes twenty-five hours to get home. It was a mixed train with hogs, sheep, and lumber. On the back were two passenger cars: a coach and a Pullman.

The plane was a two-seat Stimpson Detroiter with space in the back for mail. The runway in Billings was quite short, on a butte overlooking the river. I said to him, "What if this damn thing don't take off?" He said, "The Yellowstone River will break the fall."

We flew over the Crow Reservation and I saw something of interest and opened the window to take a better look. I pulled my head back in and asked the pilot, "Did I have glasses on?" I thought maybe I left them at the hotel. ... He said, "You had them. Where are they?" I said, "Down on the reservation."

That plane had to be refueled every couple of hours, so we flew to Sheridan, then to Casper, and then to Cheyenne. In Cheyenne I phoned Bea at the Park Lane Hotel to pick me up at the airport. I said, "I am in Cheyenne and will be there in fifteen minutes." She said, "You will kill yourself driving that fast." She had no idea I was flying.

Papa Jack told this story to his great-grandson Colter's third grade class at Denver's Polaris Program at Ebert Elementary School. The following drawing was made by a student who had listened to the story.

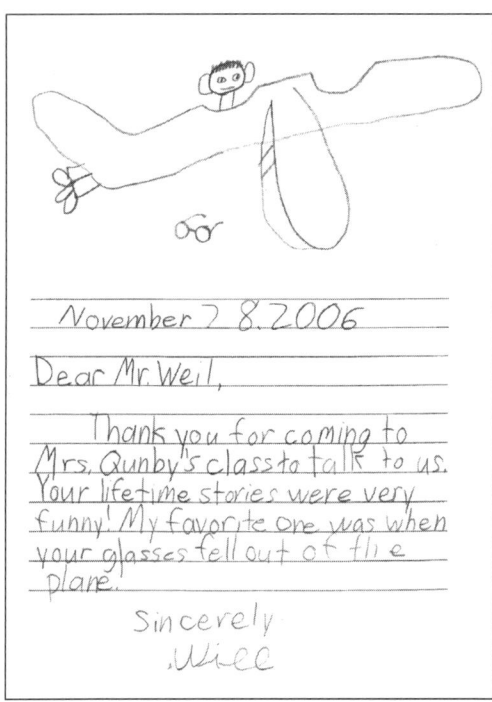

◆ ◆ ◆

◆ Papa-isms

"Every time I sassed someone, Papa would say, 'Are you looking for a scab?'

"Another thing he said, when people reference the past and its no longer true: 'Was ain't is.'

"Often the skeptic, he would say, 'Who guarantees the guarantor?'"

—Gail Sigman, granddaughter

◈ On Bad Deals
"Whenever Papa felt a deal was bad, he would say, 'They are giving you everything the chicken laid but the egg.' "
—Jane Romberg, daughter

◈ Cold Cash Jackson
Sam Kornblatt first worked with Papa Jack in the 1940s at Miller & Company, located in downtown Denver. Later, Sam became one of Rockmount's first employees. He worked with Papa for over sixty years.

Not long ago, I bought a mirror with an inscription from Mattie Silks, the storied nineteenth-century brothel on Denver's Market Street in LoDo. This prompted Papa Jack and Sam to tell a colorful story.

Papa Jack reminisced, "Before I got into the western wear business, I was a salesman and opened an office in the Interstate Trust building at Sixteenth and Lawrence. It was across the street from the Golden Eagle (where he and Sam later worked at Miller & Company).

"There was a guy on the corner with a ready-to-wear store. His customers were women that worked in the whorehouses."

Sam recalled his name: "Cold Cash Jackson."

> Papa Jack "fell in love with the Western way of life." His trademark saying was "the West is not a place, it's a state of mind."
> —*Colorado Business*, October 1993

Papa continued, "He took dresses to them to try on and if they liked them they bought them ...

"He had a girl working in the store. One day a guy from Lowry Air Force Base needed a ride back to the field. Jackson had the girl drive the guy in his new Buick. The next thing Jackson got was a telegram that they went to Chicago ..."

Sam added, "The guy still had the store in the '50s, even the same customers ..."

◆ Behind Every Great Innovation,
There is a Dream, Vision, and Passion

This is a story about a man who learned how to work as a child. His family had a milk cow and his first job was delivering milk to the less fortunate using a goat wagon. Later, as a teen, he delivered the *Evansville Courier* newspaper. He did well and went on to manage the distribution of the papers among the other carriers. He gave his brother Edgar the first papers off the press and they delivered them downtown first, then went to a home route. In high school, during World War I, he worked afternoons as a quality inspector at the D.S. Bernstein Overall Factory, which made dungarees for the U.S. Navy. There he learned apparel manufacturing, which became important later in his long life.

Papa put up the Paris Garter sign at his office at Sixteenth and Glenarm in 1928. Courtesy Denver Public Library, Western History Collection.

Papa Jack came out West with his new bride Bea in 1928. He arrived looking for opportunity, the same as pioneers and miners before him and every transplant since. It was not the get-rich-quick story of the gold rush, but hardworking perseverance from the midwestern work ethic that he brought from Indiana, rooted in his family's French and German upbringing.

Papa was sent to open a sales office for A. Stein & Company, which sold Paris Garters. He had an office at Sixteenth and Glenarm.

He met the Miller family and became friends with Phil Miller. Phil asked him to become his partner and the two built the first company dedicated exclusively to Western apparel. When Papa joined the company it was primarily a jobber of other brands. Papa built the design and manufacturing side.

◈ Too Many Hats

Papa Jack liked to tell the story of an Elks Convention that came to Denver in the 1930s. The buyer at the Denver Dry Goods Store ordered thousands of hats for them. "Ten thousand Elks came to town and ten thousand Elks left without a hat." The buyer was frantic, and thought he would lose his job. Papa and Phil Miller took out little ads in country newspapers advertising the hats. Later on, people wanted other things besides hats. And that is what got Miller off the ground and into wholesale in a bigger way.

They prospered during the Depression, as the rural West fared better than the large urban areas on the coasts. Much of their business was with big chain stores. Papa preferred special treatments and better quality than the chains wanted, so he left to start Rockmount in 1946. His most famous innovation came at this time—the first shirts with snaps.

Little did he know that his original regional market would one day span the globe.

CHAPTER 3

Papa Jack's Unique Sense of Humor

◆ How Do You Feel?

Never one to say the obvious, Papa Jack answered the most mundane questions with irony. He would show his quick wit when a customer asked, "How do you feel?"

"With my fingers," Papa Jack would always respond.

◆ The Computer

Many people are surprised that Papa Jack used a computer. Someone once asked him, "Do you use the computer at your desk?" Papa, blue eyes peering through wire-rimmed glasses, answered, "What the hell would I do without it?"

◈ The Deer Head

Papa Jack had a deer head on the wall behind his desk since he started Rockmount. When we were kids, he told us the rest of the deer was on the other side of the wall. In those days Colorado Tent & Awning, owned by the Getchell Family, was next door to Rockmount. We went over there more than once looking for the rest of the deer.

◈ Telling the Mundane

Once, Papa had a bruise and someone asked, "How did you get that bump on your head?"

He replied without hesitating, "I thought my wife said 'stand up,' but she said 'shut up'!"

Papa Jack, ever humorous, never missed the chance to spin an amusing story rather than tell the mundane.

Frequently people asked him, "Have you lived in Denver all your life?" His usual refrain: "Not yet."

◈ Attitude

Gerard Rudofsky from Zaidy's Deli, where Papa and Dad had brunch most Sundays for many years, had this to say about Papa. "He had a great attitude. When he'd come into Zaidy's, I'd ask him, 'How are you doing?' He'd say 'Compared to what?'"

❖ Answering the Phone

How many presidents answer their company phone? Papa Jack didn't need focus groups to stay in touch with his customers. He did it the old way. When the phone rang, he was often the first to answer it. People often expressed surprise at this and asked, "How come *you* answered the phone?" His reply: "It rang." His modesty is a lesson to all of us.

❖ When Meeting Pretty Women

Never short for a good opening line, Papa Jack often said: "Where were you when I was your age?"

He was a charmer. More then once, when a pretty woman came out of the dressing room, and Papa Jack was asked: "Do you like my shirt?" He replied, "I like what's inside." He liked telling women he thought they were pretty with or without the shirt.

When other employees would help young women, Papa Jack often kidded that so and so "only helps the pretty ones …"

Gretchen Bun, a friend of the family, once told my grandmother Bea that she had a crush on Papa Jack. My grandmother took it fine. Gretchen said, "When I told him how cute he was, he replied 'Now you tell me. Why didn't you tell me twenty years ago?' He was a darling. I loved flirting with him. He flirted 'til the day he died. He was adorable. I miss going to lunch with him."

❖ On Birthdays
I stopped celebrating birthdays; now I observe them.

Papa Jack and Steve Weil at Seventeenth and Wazee, celebrating street sign change for Papa's 106th birthday, March 28, 2007.

❖ Will We still Get Our Mail?
"In honor of Papa Jack's one-hundredth birthday, the city of Denver began temporarily renaming Wazee Street as 'Jack A. Weil Boulevard' each year. Papa commented, 'I think it's a lot to do about very little. Do you think we'll still get our mail?'"

—The Denver Post, January 11, 2001

❖ Discipline
"He used to tell me he was going to give me a spanking when he got home from work. He said, 'I don't know what you did wrong, but you'll know.' He actually never laid a hand on me."   —Jane Weil Romberg, daughter

❖ How to Keep the Sun Out of Your Eyes
Papa Jack had a practical approach to life. "I always live east of where I work so I don't have the sun in my eyes driving to work or back home."

CHAPTER 4

On Romance

To me, coming to Colorado was a romance.
—*The Rocky Mountain News,* January 11, 2001

TELL US ABOUT YOUR FIRST ROMANCE, HOW YOU MET GRANDMA

There was a convention between Christmas and New Years of the Pi Tau Pi Fraternity in Memphis.* This girl lived in a town 85 miles from Memphis and met my brother Edgar. He told her that his brother was going to be down there after the first of the year. I did not want to go, was glad to stay home.

* Joan Weil thinks Papa was the last surviving member of *Pi Tau Pi*. Joan is the daughter of Bill Drucker, Papa's first business partner in the early 1920s. She married Papa's nephew Leo.

I had traveled Michigan to Pittsburgh. A. Stein & Company sent me to Memphis and extended my territory . . .

We made arrangements to meet at the Claridge Hotel. Well, I was not sure about what kind of deal my brother was setting me up for. Before I had a chance to call her, she called me. She was visiting some relative. (In the South they were all kinfolk.) So she said she could come downtown to meet me. I thought she was an eager beaver and she said, "How will I know you?"

I looked around and there was a guy sitting in the lobby reading a paper. So I told her I was dark complexioned with a heavy beard, and she would recognize me. I was describing the guy sitting in the lobby. [chuckles]

There was a mezzanine above the reception desk. I went up there to stand and see what she looked like because I was not sure what my brother was giving me.

I stood on that balcony and she walked in the front door, took a look at that guy I had described, hesitated, and then went to the front desk. By the time she got to the desk I was down below. She said, "Surprising me like that was the worst thing ever done to me." That was Bea.

She stayed there at the hotel. We ate there. She ordered squab, and I said, "Are you going to eat that poor little pigeon?" She could not eat a bite! She said to me, "That is the worst thing anyone ever did to me." After all, I was a cosmopolitan from Pittsburgh and she was a country girl from the South. I was kind of independent [chuckles]. *Here was a little country girl from a town of five thousand, of which four thousand were black. They* [her family] *were the only Jewish people in town.*

[Grandma told the story of how people from all over the area came to see her when she was born. Her mother thought it was so nice that so many people came to see her little baby girl. Later, she found out they came to see her because they had never seen a Jewish baby and thought she had horns.]

I was going from Memphis to Jackson, Tennessee. The next day or two I took her to Humboldt and met her family—her mother and three brothers were living at home. (The fourth brother was living in Birmingham, Alabama. Henry Baum, the father, had died.)

The only paved road in west Tennessee was from Humboldt to Trenton, ten miles. The people would go from Humboldt to Trenton for a loaf of bread just to ride on that pavement. Those in Trenton did the same thing by coming to

Virginia Hotel
RATES $1.50 AND UP
DALEY-MOFFATT HOTEL CO.

E. S. MOREY, MANAGER

MONROE, LA.

Monday night, 6.30.

Darling Lover,

We're going swimming in half an hour, but I'm writing now so that you will get my letter on time. Milton and Isaac and I will go in for a little while before eating. It's been hot again all day, and the water will feel fine.

Lover, the invitation came today. Makes us realize that IT is really coming off. Gave me a thrill to see it, Darlin'. What about you?

And the poor neb has to address them all! Well, that's what you get for getting married.

Honey, if <u>you</u> want to send Max Good an invitation, go to it. I'm not sending them to all <u>my</u> friends, and you are. However, do add the following to the list:

Mr. and Mrs. Isaac Lemle, Mr. & Mrs. Julius Lemle,
411 Washington St., Monroe, La.

We have to do it, because both Julia and Ethel will

Papa Jack wrote his betrothed every day. This letter was written three months before their wedding.

Humboldt. Trenton had a couple of Jewish families, one named Fishman that came to Denver later, too . . .

In those days when people came to this country they landed in New York and there was an organization that dispersed people. A lot of them went to northwest Tennessee, north of Memphis. They did not speak English, they spoke mostly German and had to learn English. There was a great difference in the handling of people from Germany where they were Reform Jews as opposed to Eastern Europe where they were Orthodox . . .

Henry [Bea's father] *came over in the 1850s, was in Jackson, Tennessee—eighteen miles from Humboldt. Later, he had*

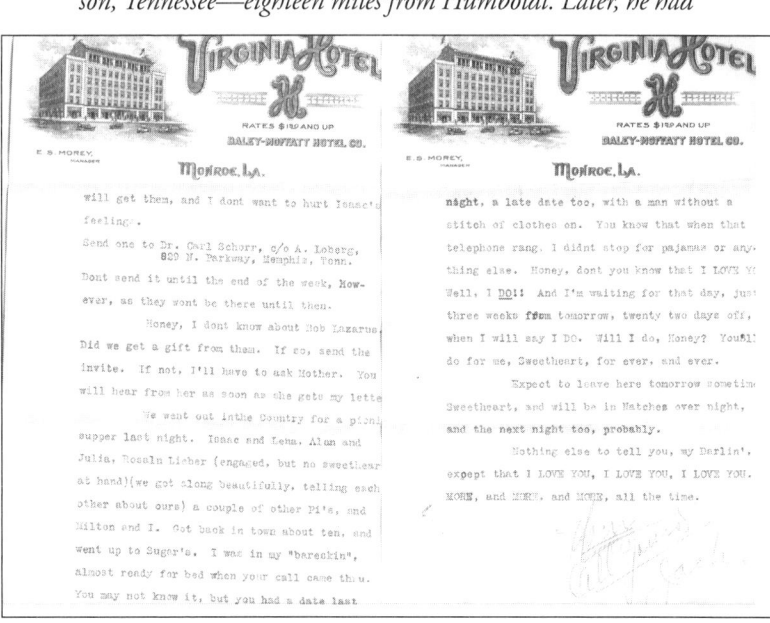

a general store in Humboldt. They bought their stock from Rice Stix Dry Goods Wholesalers in St. Louis. He married Bea's mother, Josephine, who also was from Germany.

Bea's home was near Jackson, so she rode over with me. I was driving my '26 Chrysler Roadster with a rumble seat. I had it when we got married the next year. We drove it out West, too.

When I let her out to go home I kissed her on the forehead. She said, "You are admiring my brains." That was the beginning of the romance.

This quotation reflects Papa's views:
"The South is a place where the past is not past."
—William Faulkner

◆ ARE WE REALLY MARRIED?

When we got married, Rabbi Kornfield from Memphis was on summer vacation and they had a substitute rabbi. My aunt —my mother's sister—came down from Columbus, Ohio, for the wedding. My mother and I were at the train station in Humboldt waiting for the rabbi to come from Memphis.

I described him as having a heavy beard and that he would want to know if we preferred the ceremony in broken English or perfect Hebrew.

My mother said "You are not doing this to me."

When the rabbi stepped off the train he was a neat looking guy and my mother kicked me in the shins. She said, "That is the worst trick you ever played on me."

Well the whole situation you could not conceive. They were still fighting the Civil War down there, they were never whipped, they were "overwhelmed." Every county seat had a Confederate soldier statue. I came from Indiana and the only thing I knew about the Civil War was in the history books. Those people lived it down there.

. . . The rabbi performed the ceremony and we went back to Memphis with him on the train. My car was in Memphis.

It turned out the rabbi had attended Hebrew Union College but never graduated. He was serving small towns in the South but never stayed in any one of them very long. He was not ordained.

That same guy married our good friends Henry and Leona Frankel. Her father immediately took them out south of Denver to Littleton to be remarried by a justice of the peace. They wanted to know if I wanted to do the same thing with Bea. I told them "I think we're having more fun living in sin." [chuckles] *We never were married by an ordained rabbi or civil servant.*

❖ ❖ ❖

> "Weil is in the saddle, that is . . .
> sitting behind a hulking wood desk as women
> fawn over him like a western Hugh Hefner."
>
> —NPR interview at his 106th birthday party
> with Nancy Greenleese, April 27, 2007

❖ ❖ ❖

❖ On Dating

Papa and grandma were married for sixty-four years. In the late '90s, some years after grandma's death, my wife, Wendy, and I were at McCormicks, a restaurant across the street from the Rockmount store. We ran into Papa on a date with a woman named Anita, so we joined them.

I did not know Anita and assumed they recently met. I could not have been more wrong.

Our family was very close and we knew each other's friends. When I asked how long they had known each other, Papa said, "We met in Boise while I was there on business in the '30s. Her husband's family had a chain of stores."

Anita and Papa had recently reconnected after she had moved to Denver.

While we were glad Papa was dating, we were relieved he never met Anna Nicole Smith, who had a penchant for older men . . .

CHAPTER 5

On Integrity and Values

"He's a beacon for everything this country stands for."
—Denver Mayor John Hickenlooper, *The Denver Post*, March 28, 2007

◈ What My Father Gave Me that His Father Gave Him

When Jack B. was a boy his father gave him a paperweight — a thick, glass-covered saying he had clipped from a magazine, expressing his philosophy. Dad kept it in his sock drawer until he gave it to me when I was a boy. I am safeguarding it for my son, Colter. It holds a special place in our family.

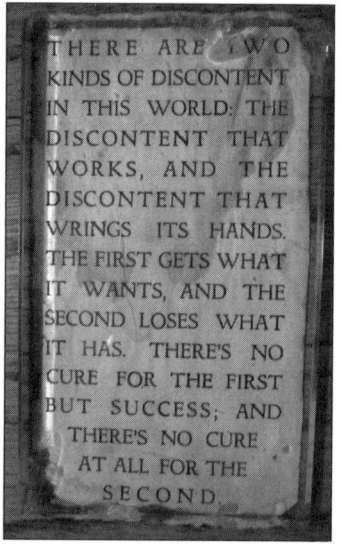

THERE ARE TWO KINDS OF DISCONTENT IN THIS WORLD: THE DISCONTENT THAT WORKS, AND THE DISCONTENT THAT WRINGS ITS HANDS. THE FIRST GETS WHAT IT WANTS, AND THE SECOND LOSES WHAT IT HAS. THERE'S NO CURE FOR THE FIRST BUT SUCCESS; AND THERE'S NO CURE AT ALL FOR THE SECOND.

◈ On Honesty

When I joined Rockmount at the age of twenty-three and applied for a credit card, I asked my grandfather, "What do I say on the credit card application about my length of employment? I have worked here since high school ..." His reply burned itself into my fiber: "Tell the truth and you'll never have to remember what you said."

◈ On Christmas Trees

The Weil family had a Christmas tree every year despite being Jewish. Many Reform Jewish families have had trees for generations. Many families brought the custom from France and Germany in the mid-nineteenth century.

Bringing an evergreen indoors around the time of the winter solstice is a pagan ritual that predates Christianity.

Papa Jack's parents Abe and Sarah Weil used to put up a tree for their grandkids when they visited. Some Jewish leaders once came to Abe and asked how, as a good Jew, he could do that. Abe responded, "How could anything that makes children happy be bad?"

◈ Principles and Practices

Known as an inventive marketer and astute businessman, Papa Jack kept his company thriving through principles and practices that he often expressed with pungency and wit. When you have been in business many years you tend to have seen it all and form ways to handle things. He had to write difficult customers from time to time. I'll never forget what he said to someone who had made false claims for shortages one too many times. We later refused to ship to them again. They wrote an irate letter, to which Papa responded, "If someone has to be mad, it's better that it be you."

We received this letter from another irate customer:

To All The Weils:

I received your bill for shipping of $12.72 for hats which I ordered in September to sell in my store in October and November, not December, which is when I received and refused them. Since your company didn't ship them on time, I feel I do not owe for any charges of any kind for your lateness.

We have done business together for some time now and if you still expect me to pay for your mistakes please cancel my account for I refuse to pay for your mistake again, as I did about 3 years ago.

Please let me know your feelings promptly.

Here's is Papa's reply:

Dear Dan:

You are correct in saying that we have done business together for some time. Do you remember that you would need take bankruptcy if I didn't take back one helluva lot of hats when the bottom dropped out? That was one pile of business in reverse!

When you ordered the hats from John the end of September, you did not specify a cancellation date, and the entire discussion is over a lousy two dozen! We both know that if you had been feeling good when they came, you would have taken them for Xmas, 2 dozen!

Now the transportation doesn't amount to the price of a good dinner and I'm charging it off. However, let us each understand each other and give and take on both ends of the stick. We each can do business without the other, it would be a sorry mess if we couldn't, but we should each benefit by doing business together, so long as it is on a mutually satisfactory basis.

I think I'm telling you how it is, and I count upon you being the kind of man to accept what is what as well.

Merry Christmas.
The old man,
Jack Weil

"For a long time, I thought he was infallible—a paragon of everything I believed in and everything I thought the world should be. I came to the realization that he was human, with human frailties and human faults. … As I began to wrap my brain around the idea that he was a person, not an ideal, my respect and admiration for him only grew and I learned from him how to be a better person…"

—Granddaughter Janet Pollack

CHAPTER 6

On Business

"When you shop Rockmount Ranch Wear,
you're shopping a Colorado institution.
Founded in 1946, Rockmount is the oldest maker
of Western shirts made in the U.S.
This three-generation, family-owned business
designed the first Western snap shirt,
which today is the longest running shirt design
in America. The first shirt retailed for $2.95;
today's snap styles range from $50 to $100
in more than 100 styles."

—*Rocky Mountain News* "Top of the Rocky," November 4, 2005

❖ On Innovation

Papa Jack didn't just create a new kind of shirt—he started a whole new fashion. He gave those who identify with the American western way of life a style tailored specifically for them. Rockmount stands out from other fashion companies because we've maintained a consistency of design for over sixty years. We go our own direction and don't look to other brands for our inspiration.

> *I was always thinking of something new. But that's me. I'm a dreamer. And I never stopped enjoying myself, not for a minute.*
> —The London Times, May 21, 2005

❖ The Shirt that Jack Built

I asked Papa Jack if, in the early days, he thought of himself as a designer or a businessman. He said, simply, "Both." He pointed out that a lot of technical details went

These shirts from the 1940s are made from rayon suiting fabrics not previously used in shirts. Fabric was another of Papa Jack's innovation in establishing a new Western fashion. He said these fabrics "made us." They were popular and helped the company get off the ground. His sawtooth pocket design became the longest-running shirt design in America, Western or otherwise. The shirts also feature shotgun cuffs and genuine mother of pearl snaps.

into making his shirts. After all, this was a new fashion, and there was no established way of producing it.

For one thing, he had to source fabrics. Some of his earliest shirts were made from rayon suitings and woolen gabardines not previously used in shirts. These fabrics were intended for other uses. Much of his genius was in reinterpreting materials and design elements in fresh new ways.

Then there were the complex manufacturing techniques necessary for creating all the special design elements and treatments in Western shirts, including flap pockets, smile pockets, fancy yokes, embroidery, and fasteners. Papa Jack personally innovated ways to manufacture this new fashion.

Innovation does not come easily. When Papa Jack conceived of a shirt with snaps in place of buttons, he approached Scovill—an industrial company that produced snaps for gloves and baby pants—and asked them to supply him. They declined. He went to the Scovill plant in Waterbury, Connecticut, to present his case. Scovill again refused, saying it was a "misapplication."

Papa Jack was perseverant and determined. He told them, "Dammit, if I bought and paid for them and ate them as Post Toasties, it's none of your business!" Senior management agreed, and together they developed snaps for shirts as well as the machinery to attach them, a relationship ongoing for over sixty years.

❖ On Protecting Your Ideas

People ask me why I never patented any of these things. Well, when I created them, a patent wasn't worth anything unless you spent millions of dollars in court. . . . And people know our merchandise is the real thing. That's why they buy it.

—*Los Angeles Times,* April 1, 2001

> **The original "Woody"?**
>
>
>
> Circa 1950, Papa Jack had "Mr. Walnut Head" made by a shoe repairman named Goldstein in Cheyenne. The dolls were made from leather scrap, and we sold them with or without a saddle. The original wholesale cost of the doll was $4.50. The saddle cost $1.75. We sold hundreds. Perhaps Mr. Walnut Head was the inspiration for "Woody" in *Toy Story?*
>
> This doll was found in an antique store in Denver and presented to me by Reed Weimer and Chandler Romeo for my fortieth birthday in 1997.

❖ Stay True to Yourself

While many competing clothing brands survive by knocking each other off on a daily basis, Papa Jack promoted the development of something new. Both he and my father taught me that a distinct and original design is our lifeblood, that the beauty of Western is very individual. The whole point of the lifestyle Rockmount represents is a rebellion against conformity. So, shopping other brands and being a follower is anathema. Our devotion to individuality is what makes Rockmount unique.

◈ On Knock-Offs
Over the years Rockmount has been copied countless thousands of times. One time Papa Jack recalled a visit from a competitor who spotted a sample Rockmount shirt made of mattress ticking. Rockmount decided against producing the shirt because the print on the fabric flaked. Papa Jack said that "later the competitor phoned me to say, 'You SOB, why didn't you tell me that shirt was no good?'" The man had copied the mattress-ticking fabric, "and every one came back." [chuckles]

◈ The Bolo Tie
I called it a Bola because bola in Portuguese means lariat . . . but I didn't write very plain and it came out "bolo." This was the beginning of the bolo tie.

◈ Green Before Green was Green
Being a Depression survivor and in the textile industry, waste was a sin to Papa Jack. He drove cars until they died.

Later ones looked like farm implements. He saved string. We ship customer orders in used boxes from incoming factory shipments. We've almost always had fluorescent lighting throughout the office and warehouse. I'm not sure who among us first began reusing the backside of paper that had already been printed on for internal paperwork. We all liked the idea of saving trees, but I thought we were just being thrifty, but—now we are green!

◆ Shirt Counter Cards

In the 1950s, Papa Jack introduced large counter cards featuring his men's shirts. During the 2004 renovation of the Rockmount building, we found the original artwork and samples of cards in four different colors, which were behind a cabinet in Papa Jack's office that was being removed. It was like hitting paydirt, as I had never seen them. Finally, a fifth one turned up during a book signing when a lady in the audience produced a yellow one. Her name was Sue Shapiro, and she was the artist in the '50s who created the cards.

◈ On Business Relationships

Customer Contact

Ironically, in this dehumanizing age when more and more people are losing personal contact, Papa Jack took delight in keeping in touch. In Rockmount's early years, he made lifelong friends all over the country, many of whom he communicated with only by letter or phone. Although he never met these people face to face, they developed close relationships. He loved knowing their histories and remembered many details about them. He joked that he knew the names of their dogs. He was an amazing repository of detail.

Contrary to most CEOs, who hide away in private offices, Papa Jack liked being out on the floor. Though he had a private office, he preferred working at a desk near the front door. In 2004, when we opened our flagship retail store, we reorganized the layout of the office and positioned his desk near the entrance of the store. He greeted everyone who walked in the front door, asking literally tens of thousands of walk-in retail customers, "Where are you from?" He always commented, depending on the answer, and often knew some arcane detail about the location—especially if it was a backwater. Nothing livened him up more than someone walking in that door, even at age 107!

◈ *Every* Customer is a Big Shot

Every January for over fifty years, Rockmount has thrown a market party for our wholesale customers who are in

Denver for the biggest Western industry trade show. A reporter from New York's fashion trade newspaper *The Daily News Record* once asked Papa Jack "to point out the big shots." We had buyers big and small at the party—people from all over the world. Without hesitation he replied, "Everyone here is a big shot."

> ### Ashtray Advertising
>
>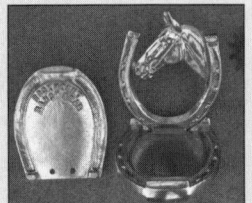
>
> Rockmount made various branded Western-style advertising pieces over the years, including ashtrays in the '50s. Papa Jack said they were Christmas gifts for dealers back when smoking was more common. The spur design was made in various finishes, including copper and gold. The horseshoe design was cast aluminum.

◆ Never Met a Discounter I Liked

One of Papa's business premises was to sell to all customers, big or small, at the same price. Although it's an industry custom to discount to larger customers, he felt that was unfair to the smaller ones. Since the 1940s, he took pride in refusing to sell to the discounters, who were responsible for the downfall of mom-and-pop stores. As for the chain stores, he said "the guy looking at the stuff, he doesn't wear it. ... Their one way of being successful is to get it for less. You can give it to them for less, but you have to take it out of the garment."

◈ How Do You *Really* Feel About Wal-Mart?

The decline of America's textile industry led Rockmount to reinvent itself. The company was wholesale for over fifty years, but has now added retail. "We never did retail because we didn't want to damage our customers," Papa Jack said. But now one giant retailer, whose name may not be spoken inside the Rockmount store, has forced many of our customers out of business.

"It's all Wal-Mart these days," Papa Jack said. "I can't stand the sons of bitches. I know all about that Walton fellow from over there in Arkansas who started it. He was nothing but a hillbilly." (*The London Time*s, May 21, 2005)

I gasped when I read this article—I had never heard Papa speak about Wal-Mart in such a way. I asked him if he had really said all those things, and he replied, "I guess I did . . ." At first I worried that they might come after us but then realized that a 104-year-old has literary license. His trademark was being forthright and telling it like it was.

In 1969, Papa Jack advanced Kay Iversen credit to open The Rockin' I Western Store in Evergreen, Colorado. In a

March 2006 *Denver Post* article, Iverson said: "He gave me $500 credit for 30 days, and I couldn't sleep all night thinking about how I was going to pay it back. He's been a great blessing to many people."

◈ On Dealing With Overdue Customers

Papa Jack had a common-man, down-to-earth approach to life. His way with people was respectful yet direct. In

business, he never forgot that people sometimes fall on hard times. Hundreds of customers have stories about how he helped them get through hard times, and credit his generosity for their comeback.

When a wholesale customer took advantage of his patience and ignored a debt for too long, Papa Jack asked him, "How long did your mother carry you? Nine months. Do you think more of me than your mother? I've carried you over a year!"

I suggest that they send me three or four checks post-dated. Not too many [business] *people do that. You have to understand your customers' problems.*

—*The Denver Post*, March 27, 2007

◈ ◈ ◈

◈ One Strategy When You Can't Collect

See these horns? How we got a pair of seven-foot horns with leather tooling:

When Steve's father got out of the service, I decided to break him in on the best bib overall and tennis shoe territory I knew—Eastern Oklahoma and Arkansas. There was a fellow there who had a gift shop and Jack B. sold him some Indian beaded belts we make here, about $35 worth. I told Jack, "We can't ship, this guy never pays a bill unless you sue him, and we can't sue him for thirty-five bucks."

Jack said, "Oh Dad, he is the nicest man, he took me to breakfast and paid for it." I said, "I guess you have to learn," so I shipped it. About four or five months later he had not paid, so I gave Jack the bill and said, "Now go get the money. You walk in that store and find something you can pick up and carry out. Start out the door with it. He'll say, 'Jack what are you doing?' You say, 'I've got this bill for you to pay. When you pay the thirty-five dollars you can have this back.'"

> *Jack picked up the seven-foot horns. But this guy says, "You want those horns for the thirty-five bucks, we'll call it even."*
>
> *Jack was driving a Ford, and that damn thing* [the horns] *was too wide to fit across the car. The only way they would go was catywampus from northeast to southwest 'til he got to Kansas City and left them at my brother's house. Later my daughter brought them home on the train . . .*
>
> *So that hangs there and whenever there is a question about somebody's credit all I do is look at it and nobody questions me from then on.* —CNN Interview, March 2001

When I asked Papa about this story, he added: *Your dad was just starting out and wasn't sure the crummy Western wear business was for him, so we didn't buy the Ford. We rented it, so we could see if it was for him or not.*

That was in 1954.

◆ On Quality
Never Buy Cheap Oats

Papa Jack loved using gimmicks to promote his business.

WE HAVE NO QUARREL WITH THOSE WHO SELL FOR LESS...THEY SHOULD KNOW WHAT THEIR PRODUCT IS WORTH. BUYING "QUALITY MERCHANDISE" is like buying oats. If you want nice, clean, fresh oats, you must pay a fair price. However, if you can be satisfied with oats that have already been through the horse...they come a little cheaper.

ROCKMOUNT RANCH WEAR

His early business cards had the standard business information on the front, but the back had a surprise.

His humor was pervasive, often earthy. He was never about price. Quality was his hallmark since the day he started in business. He never liked the chain stores because they prospered by cheapening their product.

◈ Made in USA

Papa Jack was a fervent supporter of "Made in USA."

I've always said that Western is the one true American deal. . . . While we have styles from Paris, and others from Italy, but Western wear came from this country and it went everywhere. I think it is bastardizing it to bring it in here from China, to be made cheaper there and they sell it cheaper but if the people aren't working here, they can't buy it anyhow.
—95th birthday video, 1996

We take pride in making it in this country. We would like very much to make it all in this country. It's a philosophy of self-preservation in this country, our way of life. If the people in this country earn their money here, and live here, there's a pretty good chance they will buy some of our products.
—CNN Interview, March 2001, at age 100

There are many amusing sayings displayed around the office, including one about importing: "When you import you get the goods and they get the money. When we make it in this country, you get the goods and we keep the money."

From the '60s on, we gave a lot of lip service fighting cheap imports. When NAFTA came in the gig was up. The textile industry was an early casualty of globalization. When we complained, nobody listened. It reminded me of the Lutheran minister who lamented, "When the Nazis first came for the gypsies and homosexuals, nobody said anything. Then they came for Jews and socialists, and nobody said anything. Later they came for the Catholics, and nobody said anything. Finally, they came for me, and nobody said anything because no one was left ..."

In the case of the U.S. economy, manufacturing was the first to be done away with by cheap imports. American textile, shoe, car, and steel industries were lost, and nobody said anything. Papa Jack lamented, "We would be hard put to make any of these things again in the U.S. We would be in a helluva shape if we could not get them abroad."

Well, now the service industry has been outsourced, including customer service, tech support, credit card processing, and airline reservations. The middle class got exported, and nobody said anything. Entire segments of the economy are gone. Elvis has left the building, the horse is out the barn door . . .

Is it futile for us at Rockmount to oppose these trends and continue U.S. manufacturing? Holding on to our roots at Rockmount became our salvation. Now we are virtually the last guys standing.

◈ On Sales, Marketing, and PR

Many companies have large advertising and promotion budgets, and a high percentage of their product cost is attributed to these soft costs. Not Rockmount. Papa Jack believed his products should speak for themselves. He believed in selling a product at its best value, without a margin for expensive advertising and promotion.

◈ I like It if It Sells

I began designing for Rockmount in the late 1980s. After producing my first shirt, I took it to Papa Jack for approval. Beaming, I asked him, "How do you like it?" He replied, "I like it if it sells."

◈ Where the Name Rockmount Came From

Rockmount is a contraction of Rocky Mountains.

—CNN Interview, March, 2001

Posters

Papa Jack began issuing posters in the 1950s. When we were renovating the Rockmount building in 2004, we found this fine large linen piece, which had been stored away and forgotten years ago. It is now on display in the Rockmount store.

Papa Jack included me in this one from the mid–'70s.

Later, we commissioned some posters based on paintings, including this portrait of the three generations by noted painter David Parker.

❖ ❖ ❖

◈ The Rainbow Label

Rockmount has maintained consistency in its branding and labeling throughout its entire sixty-plus year history.

This is unusual because most companies change brands and labels like the seasons. Rockmount's label is one of the longest running designs in the fashion business. The logo has remained the same, but the colors have changed

over the years. Our famous rainbow label was introduced early on, retired in the 1970s, and reintroduced in the late '80s for premium and vintage styles. These wonderful graphics, created by Papa Jack when he started the business, can't be improved upon—why change a good thing?

◆ Only in this Country

"Two signature shirts from Rockmount's collection were worn in the movie *Brokeback Mountain* and sold on eBay

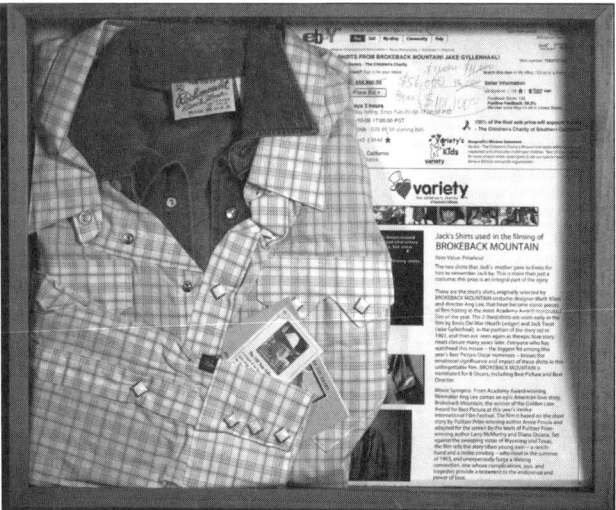

recently for $101,100.51. The money was donated to charity. 'Only in this country,' Weil said."

—The Denver Post, March 29, 2006

◆ On the Limelight

How many people do you know who have turned down appearances on the *Tonight Show* or Fox TV? Since Papa Jack turned one hundred years old, booking agents had been contacting us, trying to get him to appear on their shows. Once he was asked to go to Los Angeles to do a TV commercial for a large brokerage house on how to make your investments last if you live to be a hundred. He turned most of these offers down. He didn't need the notoriety and didn't feel the travel was worth it.

Our family and business was obscure for its first forty years or so. As Denver's historic LoDo district became increasingly popular, we became more visible due to our location there. My grandfather turning one hundred, our opening a retail store, and my book all added to this increased local profile. When, in 2005, our shirts were worn by actors in the movie *Brokeback Mountain* and by musician Eric Clapton, our notoriety became international. My father and grandfather were bemused by the attention.

We began getting frequent requests for interviews from media both major and minor. We learned to be careful in choosing who we'd work with, as a couple of times we had been burned by trusting media who had ingratiated itself with us. We also didn't want Papa Jack to be overburdened. Getting around became a challenge for him in later years. His rest was paramount, so we were protective about these claims on his energy.

Papa Jack didn't have a problem with the media attention. He told me, "Don't be a big shot." He had a terse way of summing things up . . .

◈ The *Tonight Show*

The booking agents for the *Tonight Show* had been after Papa Jack since he turned one hundred years old. We heard from them every year, asking if he would go to L.A., and every year we turned them down. Eventually, I suggested they fly him privately so he could avoid the airport hassles. The agent said, "Richard Gere is not flown privately." I replied, "Fine, Richard Gere is not over one hundred years old." Then I suggested they come to us. They agreed, and arranged for Mo Rocca to interview Papa at Rockmount.

When the crew arrived in July of 2007, I told Mo my only request was that he not make fun of my grandfather. He said, "No problem," and opened the interview by asking Papa Jack, "Who do you prefer, George Bush or Grover Cleveland?" The interview went downhill fast, and Papa Jack did not tolerate being made to look silly. Most of our media experiences proved better than that one.

◈ Don't Try to "Handle" Papa Jack

Papa Jack was a natural. He wasn't about image and needed no public relations firm. In 2006, *CBS Evening News* asked for an interview during a week I had to be away at a trade show. I asked Gretchen Bunn, a former media executive now working in our retail store, to help prepare my grandfather for the interview.

Gretchen recalls that she "asked Papa Jack if he would like to wear a new, colorful, vintage embroidered shirt." Always independent, he responded, "No, what do I look like, a rookie? I'll wear the blue plaid I wear all the time."

She then tried to give him some talking points. In her prior career in cable television she dealt with the media a lot. She said, "If I thought picking out his clothing was hard, trying to influence what he was going to say was *impossible*. I went on for ten minutes about how he would have to speak carefully and concisely for sound bites. There would be very little time to promote the company. He finally stopped me and said, 'They are going to be here for hours interviewing me and will edit it down to a few lines, whatever it is they want to air. Leave me alone!' "

Gretchen's conclusion: "Papa Jack can not be 'handled.' By the way, the interview went fine ..."

◈ On Building a Successful Business

◈ ◈ ◈

I started Rockmount because I wanted to maintain certain ideals I thought a business should have.

I was never going to have a customer give me over five percent of my business, and that way if I lost them I wasn't going to bleed, and they could not influence me on the quality of what I did.

I was never going to tell a customer how many items are in a box. A customer should buy what he wants. We were selling an idea of turning your goods.

There never was going to be a difference in the price to anybody, whether a merchant buys a little or a lot. We have no inside prices. We will never be the biggest frog in the pond. We have close personal friends all over the world who are our customers. —95th Birthday Video, 1996

◈ ◈ ◈

◈ Eighty Percent of Success is Showing Up

Woody Allen once said that "Eighty percent of success is showing up." Papa Jack showed up every day of his ninety-plus-year working life. His work ethic is legendary.

Vision and entrepreneurial spirit are what it takes to start a business. Yet it takes more than good ideas to perpetuate one. Small businesses survive because of commitment, hard work, and resilience to setbacks. Those that survive the longest have overcome the most. It's all about attitude. Do you work to live or live to work?

Running your own business is both a burden and a privilege. The added burden is that you take your work home with you; it is never merely a forty-hour-a-week job. Papa Jack believed that if you do what you like, it's not work. Controlling your own destiny is perhaps the core benefit that makes working for yourself so deeply satisfying.

When giving advice to people about choosing the right career, he would say, "Pick a job you love. There is no more drudgery than a job you disdain." His work was not a job, it was a romance.

"As for his success in business,
he advises staying out of debt—
Rockmount has always been self-capitalized—
helping others to succeed alongside you,
and constant innovation."
—*The London Times,* May 21, 2005

◈ Something Unique
People want to wear something unique. And we provide it. The idea never ages. —*Los Angeles Times,* April 1, 2001

Papa Jack designed these signs, which were sent to Rockmount dealers in the 1940s and '50s. They are silk-screened on wood. When they come up at auctions, they sell for several hundred dollars.

◆ Personal Contact
I love the personal contact I've had with all kinds of people. For me, that's what always made it fun. And it never hurt to be a bit of a "ham."   —The Denver Post, June 21, 2004

◆ On Opening a Retail Store
We went into retail to stay in business. Wal-Mart has put a lot of independent merchants out of business. The wholesalers

are nearly gone. But it might be better for the consumer.
—*The Denver Post,* March 27, 2007

"Jack Weil sends out a message
of what you can do if you are willing to work.
He is a huge billboard for the American work ethic."
—Denver Mayor John Hickenlooper, CBS 4 Denver, March 2006

◈ Like What You Do

Samuel Johnson said to James Boswell in 1777, "No, sir, when a man is tired of London, he is tired of life; for there is in London all that life can afford." London for Papa Jack was his life's work. He loved his day-to-day work at Rockmount, whether handling administrative functions, greeting customers, or chatting with staff.

"'Well, if you like what you do, it isn't hard,' Jack Weil says confidently. 'He's one of those people whose existence is defined by his work,' says grandson Steve Weil, who helps run the family business along with his father, Jack B. Weil."

—9 News KUSA, Dec 9, 2004

◈ Keys to Success

- When others took on debt to grow their business, Papa Jack grew his business from its earnings.

- While other companies patronized the big discounters, he preferred dealing with small mom and pop stores.
- While others cheapened their products for higher production volume, he stayed dedicated to quality and distinctive design.
- When others continued keeping paper accounting journals, he began computerizing in the 1960s. His first computer processed punch tape, his most recent was Windows based.
- When most CEO's chose to be insulated and out of public sight, he chose to be the first person people saw when they entered the building.
- When others retired, he continued working.

A Bigger Pen for Bigger Business

These novelty pens are twelve inches long, and were handed out in the 1940s when Papa Jack first started Rockmount. They are the only three surviving examples I have seen.

◈ ◈ ◈

◈ His Mistress: The Business

"Life may not last forever, but Papa Jack Weil plans to be at Rockmount as long as it does.

"'My wife (who died 20 years ago) always said this business was my mistress. I think she was right.'"

—*Cowboys & Indians Magazine,* June 2006

CHAPTER 7

On the Western Business

*I've always believed we were never selling just the cowboy—
we were selling the romance of the West. That's so much more.*
— Western & English Today, March, 2001

◈ Building the Western Market

"Ranchers and cowboys 'wore overalls when they worked, but they wanted colorful stuff when they came to town,' he said.... He realized his market had to expand beyond working ranch hands.

"'The cowboy business wasn't an industry,' he said. 'There wasn't enough of them, and they didn't make enough money. They'd come to town, get drunk and the next month do it again. I felt there was a market from

Middle Westerners and Easterners and we could take advantage of the popularity of Western movies. In the East you had to make it casual wear. I saw an opportunity to make a difference.'"

—Rocky Mountain News, January 11, 2001

◆ Promoting a New Fashion

I had the idea that the best place to start was at Cheyenne Frontier Days. I talked to the chamber of commerce. The Union Pacific pulls two trains a day through Cheyenne. We got them to offer a stop for the day so people could go to the rodeo. I got the town to dress up, they had to be Western. We suggested kangaroo courts for people who were not dressed Western. It was a great gimmick.

◆ No Westerner Like an Easterner

Papa Jack was fond of saying "there is no Westerner like an Easterner." When he started in business, the market for Western wear was the West. When people from the East visited or came to a dude ranch they wanted to take something home. This is how Western fashion originally made its way across the country.

◆ Shirt Design

Papa Jack was to Western shirts what Henry Ford was to cars. He was a pioneer of Western fashion and was integral to popularizing it. When he began in business in the '30s, the market for Western wear was the Rocky Mountain West.

When Papa started Rockmount in 1946, he did all of the design and manufacturing until his son, Jack B., joined the firm in 1954. My dad headed design and merchandising for over thirty-five years. His dad was a tough company founder and not open to others helping him do his job. So my dad had to earn his stripes. Dad said he had "designed the line in his head for years" until he was finally allowed to do the real thing.

When the international business started to develop, they wanted new designs. That is how I got started doing my own collection. I had helped my father design for years, but I had not done it independently until the late '80s. By the mid–'90s, I took over the design department, and continue to do all the design today.

◈ Bolos and Hat Brims

"To understand the western style, he sat through countless western movies. The motion picture cowboys of the '30s and '40s wore those thin ties with the long tails—string ties. The ties inspired Weil to make the first western bolo tie. . . . He thought the motion picture cowboys' flat-brimmed hats 'made 'em look like yay-hoos,' so he came up with the idea of curling the brims up. He told everyone it was so four cowboys could sit across in a pickup truck."

—*American Cowboy* magazine, January/February 1998

❖ ❖ ❖

"Ms. Allen (costume designer for *Brokeback Mountain*) used shirts from Rockmount, which pioneered snap-front shirts and sawtooth-style pockets in the late 1940s, and is one of the last 19th-century Western-wear companies still in operation. Today Rockmount does a much bigger business in relaxed-fit shirts for cowboys riding the range in a Tahoe."
— *The New York Times,* March 9, 2006

❖ On Going into the Western Business

I didn't know anything about the business, but I knew what I wanted. In my love for the country and its potential, I figured we had a product. I knew how I felt about it. I knew about the romance of the country.

—Westword, March 15, 2001

"Rockmount is an American icon
that has survived the 50-year decline of the
[Western fashion] industry. It has prospered while
giants such as Levi Strauss have suffered."
—*The London Times,* May 21, 2005

❖ ❖ ❖

❖ What is it About the Western Look that Appeals to People?
It's still a concept of what our country was not too long ago. We're still a young nation. . . . The West is a state of mind. Western wear has endured because of the romance of it.
—CNN Interview, March 2001

❖ ❖ ❖

"I recently bought some of your shirts from a friend of mine on Kings Road in Chelsea, England, and was knocked out. I've always loved real Western clothes and have found it increasingly hard to find them, even though I have toured extensively across the states for the last

40 years. ...

"You'll be pleased to know that we just played the first of four Cream reunion gigs in London at the Royal Albert Hall, and I was wearing one of your shirts. The last show is on Friday, so with any luck I can wear one of the new ones."
—Eric Clapton, May 2005

◈ ◈ ◈

◈ The Allure of the Cowboy

"Pausing from work, his grandfather mused that he struck it rich by picking a business that everyone could love.

"'I guess I was just lucky that every kid wants to be a cowboy,' he said."

—Reuters worldwide syndicated news story, April 6, 2006

In October 2007, Scott Pelley interviewed Bruce Springsteen on CBS's *60 Minutes*. Pelley conducted the interview  wearing a classic Rockmount denim shirt, so I contacted him. Scott replied, "I've been buying Rockmount shirts from the Denver store for many years. I have a wardrobe of them. Jane wants me to throw out the ones with holes in them, but I refuse. ... I often give Rockmount Ranch Wear as gifts."

◈ How the Sawtooth Pocket Came About

"Rockmount's signature design is the longest running shirt in America. 'The secret is to have something other than the run of the mill. ... The sawtooth pocket evolved so that we could put two snaps on it instead of one.'"

—CNN interview, March 2001

❖ ❖ ❖

"As they stood together, three generations of
Western design stood with them—Jack A. Weil
with his traditional plaid saw-toothed shirt,
son Jack B. Weil in a brownish rough cotton shirt
with 'smile' pockets, and grandson Steve with
embroidery around his sea-green shirt."

—*Los Angeles Times,* April 1, 2001

❖ ❖ ❖

❖ Luck and the Snap-front Shirt

"'I guess I was just lucky. Better that than smart.' Papa Jack is talking about his career in fashion. Yes, fashion. He's the man who invented one of the great American iconic pieces of clothing. The snap-front Western shirt.

"'He says he made it so cowboys couldn't get hung up on their saddles. I think it was a success because cowboys didn't like, or know how, to sew on buttons.' That's his grandson Steve Weil explaining the business to me while we walk around the company store in downtown Denver.

"'I can't believe what he did,' Steve Weil says as we look down from the balcony overlooking the store. Jack is in an animated conversation with someone who has walked in. Yes, animated at 106. Yes, he uses a computer."

—CNBC, December 5, 2007

◈ Why Buy an Old Shirt?
"His [Steve Weil's] 103-year-old grandfather doesn't understand all the fuss with expensive vintage shirts. He remembers when shirts sold for $45 a dozen and can't fathom why someone would spend $100 for an old one."

—*The Denver Post*, December 13, 2004

Beginning in the 1980s, I began displaying the ancient Rockmount shirts I had collected since high school. The term vintage clothing was not in use yet. I had removed some shirts from my grandfather's closet that dated back to the '40s. My desire to preserve history by hanging these shirts in our lobby museum ran counter to his desire to stay warm. More than once our lobby would have an empty hook where a shirt had been removed on cold Colorado winter days. He would take my exhibits home to wear. For him these forty-year-old shirts were meant to be worn; for me, to preserve.

CHAPTER 8

On Driving

PAPA JACK'S DRIVING is the subject of folklore. Anyone who went for a long drive with him never forgot it. People across the country recount perilous drives to the mountains. When you consider the way he drove, his longevity was a miracle.

Whenever anyone said anything about his driving he would typically say, "I've been driving since before you were born."

For years our family tried to figure out a way to get him to give up driving without ruining his independence. Papa drove until his 103rd birthday. He would have continued driving had his insurance not canceled when he forgot to renew his license on his birthday. The insurance company would reinstate the policy for $5,000 a year. He resisted

> CNN interviewed Papa Jack on the occasion of his 100th birthday. The interviewer drove with him to work and commented, "You're a good driver." He replied, "How the hell do you think I survived if I couldn't drive?"

the inevitable loss of independence he had enjoyed for nearly ninety years. We feel very thankful that he had no serious accidents while he was driving.

In the last forty years his cars—always Chryslers—ended up looking like farm implements. They were driven hard and put up wet. You needed to wipe the back seat before sitting on it. The headliner of the car dropped like a curtain between the front and back seats…but he never used the rear-view mirror anyway.

◆ On the First Cars

My father was in the cattle business and we had a horse and buggy. We'd ride beside the river to cool off, and here would come one of those horseless carriages with a spare tire. My father would say, "I never needed a spare leg for my horses."

My first car was a Model "T" Ford roadster with wire wheels. Edgar and I paid $50 for it. We were in high school. The wheels had a screw mount. When you went forward it was alright. If you backed up the wheels would fall off and *roll down the street. The car was light enough to pick up and screw them back on.*

Papa Jack told this story to his great-grandson Colter's third grade class at Denver's Polaris at Ebert Elementary School. This drawing was made by Colter.

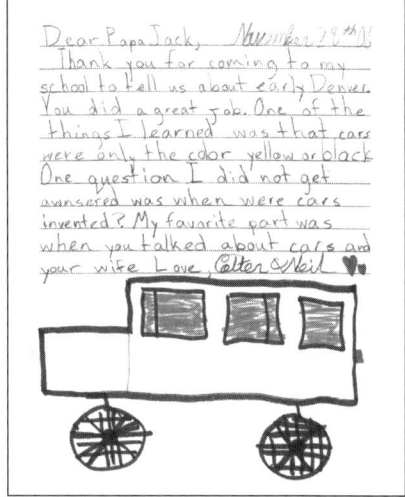

◆ You Would Do it for Me Wouldn't You?

Papa Jack was always there when we needed him. When I came home for the summer after my first year of college, I took my '58 MG to Boulder to see friends. The car had been stored in the garage all year and broke down on the way home. I left it in a parking lot and called Papa the next morning.

He offered to drive me back to Boulder and tow the car home. I asked, "Are you sure you really want to do it?" He said, "You would do it for me, wouldn't you?"

Well, we used a towrope tied to his bumper. He drove so fast, I kept tapping my foot on the brakes of my car. Finally, the towrope tore the center section out of his bumper. He drove the car like that for years.

❖ ❖ ❖

❖ The Upside-down Cake

Bea was driving with an upside-down cake sitting on the seat next to her. A police car stopped her with siren and lights blaring. She threw on the brakes and the upside-down cake went on the floor—landing upside down. So when the cop came to the door, before he could say anything, she gave him hell. "Look what you did to my cake! Did I kill someone?"

So, the cop picked the cake up off the floor and put it back on the seat. By that time he had recovered enough that he could talk to her. He said, "Lady, you are driving the wrong way on a one-way street."

She was taking the cake to patients at Fitzsimmons Army Medical Center. She'd missed the entrance and went past it into a top-secret area. It was a military police officer that stopped her. She said, "Thank goodness you found me, I'm lost." He took her to the entrance. You can take the girl out of the country, but you can't take the country out of the girl.

❖ Reinforced Concrete Columns

Everyone always blamed my grandmother for the scrapes on the car caused from hitting the concrete columns holding up the apartment building where they lived. The columns around their parking space were reinforced over the years. It was when Bea stopped driving and the car continued to get beat up that we realized she was not alone in causing the mishaps.

One time in the 1990s, I was riding with Papa Jack while he drove. The passenger-side rearview mirror was slapping the mirror of each parked car we passed. He hardly noticed, so I gently reached across and turned the steering wheel five degrees and we cleared the remaining cars on the street.

◆ A Trip to the Airport

In 1995, Papa Jack was invited to Dallas to receive the Western Industry Lifetime Achievement Award. My wife, Wendy, volunteered to drive to the airport with him. Wendy asked him, "What time should I pick you up?" He replied, "Honey, I've been driving longer than you have. I'm going to pick *you* up."

Wendy continued with the story. "He and his daughter, Jane, picked me up. He drove, barely showing over the steering wheel. The sun was in his eyes. Suddenly, he let go of the wheel with both hands to look for his sunglasses. Luckily Jane was next to him and grabbed the wheel.

"At the airport he quickly found a parking space in the front row, saying proudly, 'I get the best spots because of this handicap tag.'

"We slowly made our way through airport security. He had to remove his boots, belt, bolo tie, hat, and all his pocket change. A passenger walked by and said, 'There is

Jack Weil, being held up for all his money.' If *that* wasn't enough, the female security guard asked him to pull out the waistband of his pants so she could put the wand down his pants. He retorted, 'You sure are nosy, aren't you.' We all laughed."

◈ On Driving at Age Ninety-nine
"In later years, more than one person expressed surprise that he still drove to work. He merely replied, 'How else do you think I'd get here?'"

—*Rocky Mountain News,* Jan 11, 2001

◈ Electric Windows
The last time I rode with Papa, I had my elbow on the door with my fingers on the gutter above the open window. I guess he did not like the wind blowing, and without saying anything he closed the window on my fingers. I screamed, "OPEN THE WINDOW!" He was puzzled. "Why all the commotion?"

◈ Air Bags Can Get in the Way
The family quietly plotted how to get Papa to stop driving. When he was in his late nineties, he called me one morning at the office and asked, "Would you come pick me up at the body shop? The air bag deployed while I was on my way to work."

He'd had an accident. This situation gave us the opportunity to address the issue of his driving. I called my Aunt Jane and said, "I think we have our way to get him to stop driving if we don't get the car fixed."

When I picked him up, a man came up to me and said he was so grateful Papa was not hurt. It turned out *the accident was not his fault!* The car was fixed, yet one more time, and he kept driving . . .

CHAPTER 9

On Life

◆ A Contrarian

Papa Jack was a contrarian and took great delight in it. His secret genius was probably in seeing things differently than the crowd. He lived that way, too. He never needed to impress people with status symbols.

In religion, he practiced his version of Reform Judaism, but deeply understood other people's beliefs. He quit one temple when it became too conservative and helped build another. He eventually returned to the first one.

While others typically take on debt to buy a house, he rented until he saved enough to pay cash.

When there was gasoline rationing during World War II, he quit the social club in the suburbs several miles from home, and started one in town.

When the trend was to buy smaller import cars, he stayed with his Chryslers.

When the trend in LoDo was for wholesale companies to sell out to developers, he said, "The only way I am leaving is feet first."

◈ Never Take out More than Three Screws

My earliest memories of my grandfather were of going through his dresser drawers and exploring all the cool things he kept. When I was about four years old, he gave me an Ingersoll "Dollar" pocket watch from the early

1900s. It was broken. He knew I wanted to see how it worked by taking it apart. We share a strong mechanical aptitude. He warned me "not to take out more than three screws from the works."

The next day, after I took out four screws, the spring blew countless parts all over the place. I collected whatever I could and called him. "Papa, if I had another pair of hands we could put this thing back together." He used to tell this story and laugh and laugh. The watch still sits in a pile in a box in my drawer.

I Consider Myself Lucky

I think I am very lucky that I am one of very few that never had to ask anyone for a job. My first job was working in an overall factory after class during high school. Then I worked there full time in 1919. Dave Bernstein offered me $18 a week. My Dad said, "Dave if he's not worth $25, he's not worth anything." Dave said alright, so that was my first real job.

I never had to look for a job. Jobs came my way until I started Rockmount and created my own job.

> "By sharing your wisdom and experience you continue to serve as a role model for future generations."
>
> —President George W. Bush, March 22, 2006

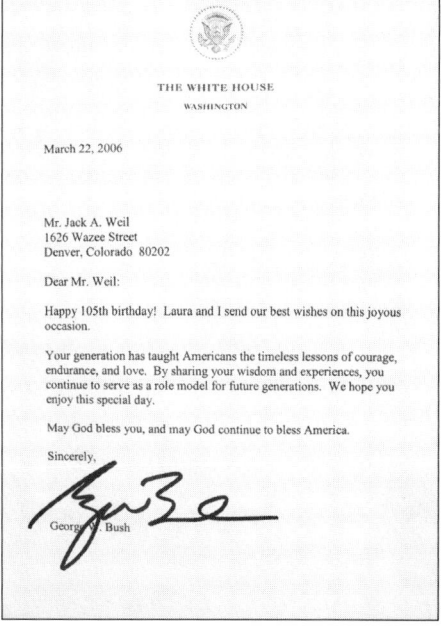

◈ Who Would Want to Live Around Here?

Papa Jack made some of his best investments inadvertently. He rarely, if ever, bought anything on credit. He bought what he could afford. When he bought the Rockmount building, it was an old warehouse in an unpopular declining commercial area, skid row.

Decades later, in the early 1980s, he was amused that people wanted to come down here to the area's bars, restaurants, art galleries, and hotels. I tried to buy a floor of the building and build a loft in the mid–'80s. He would not hear of it. Later, when Coors Field was built nearby and lofts became pervasive in the '90s, he was still perplexed that anyone wanted to live in this old neighborhood.

That his old warehouse, built in 1909, turned out to be architecturally significant—a prime example of Prairie Style modern architecture—was a pleasant surprise. We loved the building, but did not know it was designed by Fisher & Fisher, Denver's leading architects for fifty years. The building became key to our brand identity and future business model. Yet another testament to his good business judgment.

◈ On Investing in the Stock Market

I don't think you can win playing another man's game. I have invested in my own game and done okay. (As recalled by Gordon and Teri Appell, family friends.)

◈ On Money and Politics

I've always felt that a young man worth his salt is a Democrat until he makes a little money. And if he wants to save that money, he becomes a Republican.

—*The Denver Post*, March 27, 2007

◈ Making Lemonade When You Have Lemons

When a tornado wiped out our shirt factory of fifty years in Ft. Smith, Arkansas, in April 1996, we had no idea the disaster would morph into an opportunity. After settling the insurance claim, which was a major loss and disruption of business, I asked my grandfather about different options for investment. I was looking at another brand to merge into our operation. He said, "The real money in this country was made in real estate."

This gave me the idea to try to buy the Rockmount building from the family. I owe him both for having bought it in the first place, and also giving me the idea to try to keep it for the business.

He often talked about how the prices of the buildings in the neighborhood had gone up and down over the years. They had been declining for decades, up until the '80s when they spiked with the oil boom. We had unsuspecting realtors and would-be investors walking in repeatedly to inquire if we would sell. His answer: "Not everything is for sale." You have to admire his stubbornness. Things would be very different without his staying power ...

He only wanted what he needed to run a stable business, without overburdening it with debt. He said, "I never wanted to be the richest guy in the cemetery."

◆ Charity, an Upbringing Over a Hundred Years Ago

Papa Jack learned charity as a child. His family had a milk cow behind their house in Evansville, Indiana. Jack and his brother Edgar had a goat cart. It was the "Big Wheel" of the early 1900s, fun with a social contract. The boys used the cart to deliver milk to needy families each week.

Sarah, Papa Jack's mother, never turned away a hungry soul. They lived near the train tracks and plenty of "hobos" stopped by. Their home was known as a place for those in need to get a bite to eat.

One time, during World War II, a German immigrant came by the Weil's home, asking for a donation. He wanted to get enough money to go fight *on the side of Germany.* Papa Jack laughed when he described his mother chasing the immigrant out of the yard with a cane!

Papa Jack began the tradition that everyone at Rockmount donate half a percent of their monthly salary to the United Way. While he ran a small business, there was always money to distribute at the end of each year as a bonus to his employees.

CHAPTER 10

On Longevity

PEOPLE OFTEN TELL me "you must have good genes." I always reply, "No, it's really the shirts." Genes help, but lifestyle has a lot to do with it. What were Papa Jack's secrets for living so long? I credit his longevity to his loving his work, living moderately, not overeating, and controlling stress by not letting things get to him.

My father lived to be 91. My genes are good. I was athletic as a kid. I grew up in a town with a lot of Germans, and there were several turnvereins [gymnasiums]. *I didn't smoke until I was 40, and I quit when I was 60.*

—*The Rocky Mountain News,* January 11, 2001

◆ On Moderation

Unless you experienced the privations of the Great Depression and World War II rationing, it is hard to appreciate their effects. When the banks failed during the Depression, Papa Jack was a young, married man. Although he lost his savings, including wedding gift money, he remained working and was better off than many. This is perhaps why he lived a comfortable yet modest lifestyle for one hundred plus years.

◆ On Smoking, Eating, and Drinking

Papa had midwestern sensibilities—he was modest and kept things simple. About the only thing he ever did to excess was work. In all other things, he practiced moderation.

Although I had never seen Papa Jack exercise, he remained trim by never overeating. He gave up red meat when he was in his nineties.

Papa Jack stopped smoking at age sixty. His friend Doc Auer told him it would help him heal faster from a hernia operation, so he stopped. He joked later, "It's not that you live longer after giving up cigarettes, it just seems longer."

He never drank to excess. I thought I knew most of his habits, but got a surprise when he turned 106 years old. The people at Jack Daniels Distillery presented him with a special edition bottle. I assumed he never drank and offered to take it home. His reply surprised me. "I drink a shot once or twice a week."

When NPR interviewed him around the same time, he said, "My doctor tells me to take a drink once or twice a week to keep my blood thin. What the hell, I'm 106 years old and still here."

◈ Health Food

Papa Jack had not exactly followed an organic regimen. He thought salad was for rabbits. In fact, he had seen to it, for the last sixty years, that the office be stocked daily with donuts. While I had proposed switching to, or at least adding, fresh fruit, his response was "poppycock."

◈ Stay Out of the Hospital

One of his secrets for living so long was staying out of the hospital. In the past fifty years, he had only been in twice: once for a hernia, and once for an angioplasty.

◈ Go Dig 'em Up

Denver's former Mayor, Wellington Webb, would stop by Rockmount from time to time. Papa Jack's grandson Greg Romberg had been in Webb's cabinet. The mayor knew some Weil history. Once, in the '90s, he innocently asked Papa Jack, "Do you still play gin rummy with your cronies?"

Jack replied, "Mayor, do you have a shovel?" To which Webb replied, "Shovel?" Jack expanded, "If you have a shovel we can go over to Fairmont Cemetery and dig 'em up."

◆ On Memory

I have people tell me, "Your memory is wonderful." Who the hell is going to contradict me? —95th Birthday Video

◆ Life is for the Living

"Life is for the living," Papa Jack maintained. He outlived his entire generation, and some of the next. Long ago he stopped attending funerals except in special circumstances. Instead, he wrote very personal condolence notes. I kept a carbon copy of one (he used carbon paper until the day he stopped working).

```
September 29, 1986

6299-2
Ms. Shelley M. Horowitz-Koons
Western Wear Roundup
35303 Delaire Landing Rd
Philadelphia, PA    19114

Dear Shelley,

Thank you for your check for $100.35 which we are applying to
your account.

I am terribly sorry about your tragedies, and want you to know
that I sympathize with you in your grief.

We all must learn that life goes on, we must accept what occurs
and make the best of it, and live for the living.

I look forward to hearing from you again soon.

Cordially,


Jack A. Weil
ROCKMOUNT RANCH WEAR MFG CO

JAW:bal
```

◆ Well, I'm Still Here, Aren't I?

Ali Oksner, Papa's great-granddaughter, recounts this story. "I clearly remember flying in from Arizona for Papa's one-hundredth birthday as a five-year-old. Once we got to Colorado and Papa's birthday party, my family and I waited our turn to see him. Finally, we got to the front of the line. 'Hi Papa. How are you?' my mom asked. Papa gave one of his classic responses: 'Well, I'm still here aren't I?' That's when I knew that his one-hundredth birthday wouldn't be his last."

◆ What the Hell Would I Do if I Retired?

The intrepid would from time to time ask Papa Jack why he never retired. When he was age one hundred, he began replying, "What the hell would I do if I retired? I come in every morning, and after lunch we go to the bank and then to the house. I get in a good half-day's work, which is enough for me."

His attitude about retirement filtered down to Jack B., who was asked the same question by CBS Evening News in 2006, to which he replied, "How the hell can I retire? My father comes to work everyday."

"When someone gets to be as old as Papa, you kind of expect him to be around forever. Obviously, in your mind

you know that there will come a day when he'll have to go, but in your heart, it's really hard to accept."
—Granddaughter Janet Pollack

◈ On Retirement
I think I'm retired now when I work four or five hours a day instead of ten or twelve hours.

"Entering the office after driving himself to work at age one hundred, Papa Jack commented, 'I'm not as spry as I was fifty years ago, but I make it.'" [chuckle]
—CNN Interview, March 2001

"People ask, 'Why the hell are you working?'
Papa Jack responded,
'Well, you have to have something to do,'
before excusing himself to take a call on line three."
—*St. Petersburg Times*, March 28, 2006

◈ On Outlasting his Competitors
Keith Coffman, a reporter with Reuters News Agency, asked Papa Jack how he outlasted his competitors. Papa Jack replied that the reason is obvious, "because they're all in the cemetery."

◈ Papa's Secret

Granddaughter Judy Weil Oksner, and sister to Steve, was asked to write a memory of Papa for this book:

"My grandfather's contemporaries knew him as 'Jack A.,' an important distinction because my father was 'Jack B.' During the last decade of my grandfather's life, when he became a familiar figure through the frequent media attention focused on his long life and his distinctly American business, many people came to think of him as 'Papa Jack' or even plain 'Jack.'

"Now, my father was Jack. His father was 'Mr. Weil' to the Rockmount family, 'Honey' or 'You Yankee!' to my Southern grandmother, and just plain 'Papa' to my brother, my cousins, and me.

"As Papa grew older and we were out around town together, an increasing number of people asked what he attributed his longevity to. Who wouldn't want to know Papa's secret to a long life in remarkably good health, with intellect and humor intact? He usually had a quick response, rarely a serious one. In recent years, he replied that he drank a few shots of whiskey every week to keep his blood thin.

"My personal theory was that if Papa's driving didn't kill him, nothing would ... and I'm not just referring to the fact that he refused to stop until he was 103 when his insurance rates soared. I never knew how nervous my mother felt about Papa's and my afternoons together until I carried my own newly minted driver's license and we headed into the Rockies, our destination unknown. 'You drive,' my mother said. 'No, let Papa drive. Never mind. Don't tell me who drove.' I tried not to pick up his driving habits, but did develop his appreciation for taking back roads and just going. Even when we wound up some place familiar, he always showed me something new.

"Toward the end of Papa's life, I read his baby book. In it, Papa's mother diligently recorded details of his life from birth through high school graduation. I had seen the book before, but mostly noted what I saw as major accomplishments: a Boy Scouts award, the high school yearbook editorship, the highest score on an intelligence test. In that last week before Papa died, I noticed details. Before his fifth birthday, Papa survived nearly every disease my own children were vaccinated against. Sarah Weil's meticulous lists showed that some illnesses lasted up to a month, no doubt killing other children of his generation.

"I began to understand how Papa lived so long and so well. He found his own way. He appreciated the little things. He never quit. And he enjoyed the ride."

◆ Life Lessons
"We'll draw these lessons from his life: If you like whatever it is you're doing, don't stop. And try to avoid working for other people." —*Rocky Mountain News,* March 29, 2001

◆ ◆ ◆

Despite outliving everyone he knew as a young man, Papa never dwelled on sadness. When Bea, his wife of sixty-four years, died in 1990, we were very concerned about its impact on him. But true to his nature, he was resilient and went on with life and work.

He outlived everyone, including his son. After Dad was diagnosed with cancer in May 2007, the family chose not to burden Papa with our day-to-day worries and medical ups and downs. We answered his questions and tried to inform him and maintain their contact—which had been daily for over five decades—but avoided passing on our anxieties. As Jack B. worsened, we were uncertain what to tell Papa.

He was no dummy. He let me know he knew the situation without coming straight out and saying it. It was his way simply to ask me, "What has your father arranged with his company stock?" He finally said, "Do you know he has a place arranged at Fairmont?" This was how he told me he knew the end was close. Papa Jack always focused on matters of importance, even at age 106. The important details never slipped by him, they perhaps even sustained him.

He went through life unfettered with negative emotions. He concentrated on the positive, on the future. He always looked forward, never dwelling on unpleasant things from the past.

After Dad died, I told Papa how Dad and I talked about what he wanted at his memorial service. Dad had instructed me that he did not want a funeral, he wanted to be cremated. He told me whom he wanted to speak at his service—ten people at two minutes each. When he listed a married couple, I asked, "Do they get two minutes each?" He replied, "No, one minute." I wrote these notes on the back of an envelope, much like Dad had done his record keeping ...

So, I asked Papa what he wanted, a memorial like Dad's or a funeral. He replied, "I'll be there but won't know it."

Always thinking ahead about positive things is what kept him going. He changed the subject and said, "We should print a flier when the DNC comes to Denver in August. They need to know we are a real Western store established in 1946. You should talk to the host committee."

Papa did not quite make it to the Democratic National Convention. He died two weeks earlier after a short illness. The DNC came to Denver, and a whole lot of the visitors came to Rockmount and took something home. Papa would have been pleased, as it certainly beat his experience in the 1930s when 10,000 Elks came to Denver, and 10,000 Elks went home without a hat. It was a huge spike in business in August 2008. The last time the Democrats came to Denver was 1908. Too bad it's only once every hundred years!

◈ ◈ ◈

CHAPTER 11

Postscript
"It'll go forever if you just play it right"

So far as the future is concerned, it is incomprehensible. My father came to this country on a sailing vessel. When he died in the '40s, during the war, fighter planes were circling, being tested over that cemetery. I thought about what happened in one lifetime. It evolves fast. Who could ever have dreamed of getting in a plane and going to Los Angeles or San Francisco in an hour and a half, eight hours to be in London.

Even with our highways today, I think there is a certain tragedy that the people don't see what they went over or through. They don't get any concept of the Grand Canyon, the Rocky Mountains, a river like the Mississippi, or a dude ranch. It's lost.

If you are driving, you don't go through a city anymore. It's progress, I am not sure it's improvement.

—95th Birthday Video

❖ ❖ ❖

Reprinted from The Denver Post *editorial page, August 15, 2008, courtesy of Mike Keefe.*

❖ ❖ ❖

Papa Jack died on August 13, 2008, at the age of 107. Coverage of his death was of course covered by the Denver newspapers, but it was also carried by National Public Radio, the *Chicago Tribune, Los Angeles Times, The New York Times, The Washington Post*, and *The Economist,* to name a few. The media interest was overwhelming and came as a surprise. In fact, once the press hit, our email and the website at rockmount.com crashed from the torrent that followed. The response somehow helped validate our feelings for our special father, grandfather, great-grandfather, boss, and friend. The following headlines and excerpts represent just some of the press coverage.

Rocky Mountain News • Thursday, August 14, 2008, front page

Memorial held for Jack A. Weil 'the universal grandpa'
Hundreds honor man whose business was symbol of West
By John C. Ensslin

Jack A Weil, the oldest working CEO in America and patriarch of a LoDo clothing company that put the snap in Western wear, died Wednesday night at the age of 107.

Weil died at home surrounded by members of his family, said his oldest grandson, Steve Weil....

Since founding the Rockmount Ranch Wear Manufacturing Co. in 1946, "Papa Jack" Weil and his company have been a fixture in lower downtown. He saw value in the former warehouse district long before it became fashionable as LoDo.

With his cowboy hat, folksy manner and his favorite greeting—"Where you from?"—he welcomed everyone from truck drivers to celebrities like Elvis Presley, Bob Dylan, Robert Redford and Eric Clapton.

They all got the same friendly treatment, said Steve Weil, who went to work for his grandfather full time in the 1980s.

Status never mattered. "He didn't care about what you were, he cared about who you were," his grandson said.

His death comes about eight months after his son, Jack B. Weil, died.

The Denver Post • August 14, 2008, front page story

Rockmount patriarch "Papa Jack" a legend in Western wear

By Joey Bunch

Denver icon "Papa Jack" Weil died Wednesday. The founder and operator of Rockmount Ranch Wear was famous for greeting customers, some famous, most not, at his Wazee Street store for more than six decades.

• • •

Weil's work popularized rodeo wear across the country decades before other clothiers jumped on board.

Gov. Bill Ritter called Weil a "legendary Coloradan and a pioneering Denver businessman."

"Colorado will miss him dearly, but thanks to his family and Rockmount's unique Western fashions, his legacy will live on for at least another 107 years," the governor said.

• • •

Pat Grant, a rancher and CEO of the National Western Stock Show, said he has worn out more than a dozen of Weil's shirts over the years. He said he would never pull on another Rockmount shirt without missing his friend.

"He was proud of his family, proud of his community and proud of the longevity of his business," Grant said.

"He represented Western values. He always greeted you by standing up, giving a firm handshake and looking you in the eye, and that's part of Western culture, and a big part of who Jack was."

• • •

Mayor John Hickenlooper fondly recalled meeting Weil when the future mayor was collecting petition signatures to open his first brew pub in LoDo near the Weil's store.

Hickenlooper said Weil was not just his friend, "but a friend of the city." He said his longtime friend "loved the West."

"He's someone who is part of defining what Denver is all about," Hickenlooper said. ...

He said Weil's many accomplishments were rooted in his principles: "What matters is not who you are, but what your dreams are and how hard you're willing to work for your dreams," Hickenlooper said.

Rocky Mountain News • Friday, August 15, 2008

By Penny Parker

WEIL'S WAY: I'm sorry, but I can't believe Jack A. "Papa Jack" Weil is gone. I've always thought of him as a Timex watch . . . he just kept on ticking. So the news of his passing Wednesday night at the age of 107 shook me.

The last time I saw him was in May during Curious Theatre Co.'s annual *Denver Stories*, a series of vignettes about Denver denizens. After the mini-play about him was performed, Jack A. addressed the crowd and continued to tell stories until his grandson and Rockmount Ranch Wear President Steve Weil ended the monologue.

"Papa Jack, it's Andy Warhol on the phone and your 15 minutes are up," Steve teased. It was priceless, as was the vignette that told Jack A.'s story in 107 short plays.

• • •

A remarkable man, a remarkable life, a remarkable legacy. I will miss him dearly.

Rocky Mountain News • Saturday, August 16, 2008

A hat tip to 'Papa Jack' Weil

By Jane Hoback and Gil Rudawsky

We lost the oldest CEO in Colorado, and probably in the U.S., this week. Rockmount Ranch Wear founder Jack A. Weil died Wednesday at the age of 107.

• • •

Papa Jack's legend grew as the clock ticked on his life. In recent years, he was profiled by CBS-TV, National Public Radio and *The Wall Street Journal*, among others. An old-school businessman who valued a handshake over a complex legal contract, he also had an eye for innovation: Rockmount got its first computer in the 1960s, and it nimbly adapted when the U.S. textiles industry fell on hard times.

After five years of trying, Jay Leno finally landed Papa Jack as a guest on the *Tonight Show* in 2007. But the show had to come to Denver—in the person of Leno emissary Mo Rocca. Asked which candidate he would favor when the Democratic National Convention hits town, the playful 106-year-old replied: "None of them. I'm a Republican."

Westword • August 21, 2008

Jack A. Weil proved that the West is not a place, but a state of mind

By Patricia Calhoun

Jack A. Weil wasn't the first person to strike out for a frontier and make a life and fortune there, and he won't be the last. But he did it with style and substance and grit, in the process helping to define Denver, this center of the new West. And all that time, he just thought he was working. It wasn't until around his hundredth birthday that the city really took notice of Jack A. and started renaming a stretch of Wazee Street after him every March. The 1600 block of Wazee had changed a lot since the days when the five-story warehouse was surrounded by other wholesale operations and businesses; it was not lined with lofts and galleries and restaurants that pointed the way to Coors Field. Steve Weil, who'd joined the family business more than a decade before, persuaded his father, Jack B., and his grandfather that Rockmount should add a retail shop, and even spruce up the old space.

The result is a combination museum/Western-wear store, a must-stop for anyone visiting Denver, the most seductive tourist trap ever devised, filled with stylish boots and belts and those Rockmount shirts, the ones seen on rock stars and in *Brokeback Mountain.*

And on so many of the people who came to Jack A. Weil's memorial service this past Sunday. It was not just a well-dressed memorial service, but a real celebration. Before he passed away on August 13, Jack had lived more than 107 years, and he'd lived those years well, filling them with great stories and sayings that spilled from his grandchildren as they shared their memories. "Was ain't is," a granddaughter remembered him saying, to show how life kept moving, kept changing. But one thing didn't change: You worked. And so even as the city made "Papa

Jack" a marketing icon, even as the "country's oldest CEO" accolades started coming in, he just kept working. Jack A. would get up every morning, Steve remembered, read the obituaries, see that he wasn't in them, and go to the office.

Was ain't is, and no one would have gotten a bigger kick out of all the people who will be in Denver for the Democratic National Convention than Jack A. Weil. He would have greeted customers and told his stories and helped set the stage for the future, for a time when all things are possible. When a 107-year-old CEO can become a city's poster boy, and Barack Obama can stand in that city's football stadium to be nominated as the Democratic candidate for President of the United States.

The West is not a place, but a state of mind. And this week, it's wide open.

The Washington Post • Sunday, August 17, 2008

Jack A. Weil, 107; designed, popularized cowboy shirts with snap fasteners

By Martin Weil [no relation]

Jack A. Weil, a celebrated entrepreneur of the American West, who added snaps and snappiness to cowboy shirts and then sold those shirts to thousands who never saw the sagebrush, died August 13 at his home in Denver. He was 107. The cause of death was not reported.

As founder and head of Rockmount Ranch Wear, Mr. Weil was regarded as a successful businessman and a symbol of longevity.

Considered the Henry Ford of the western shirt and a major force behind a notably American fashion, he was also said to be American's oldest chief executive.

A visionary and a classic innovator, Mr. Weil conceived the idea more than 60 years ago, according to grandson Steve Weil, that "westerners needed their own fashion identity."

Aiming, his grandson said, to give western wear a look as distinctive as the region's topography and lifestyle, Mr. Weil created a slim-fitting shirt that in its cut and its cuffs, its pocketing and its fastenings, was to prove immediately recognizable.

Chicago Tribune • Friday, August 15, 2008

Maker of iconic cowboy wear
Denver company's snap-buttoned Western shirts have longtime following among entertainers

By Ivan Moreno

DENVER—Jack A. Weil, founder of the Rockmount Ranch Wear company whose snap-buttoned Western shirts became popular with movie stars and rock icons, has died. He was 107.

• • •

"I learned fast you can't sell to cowboys; they have no money," the elder Weil said in a 2001 Associated Press interview. "You have to appeal to the cowboy in everyone and sell to them."

Mr. Weil's shirts have been worn in movies by Elvis Presley, Clark Gable (in his last film, "The Misfits") and Heath Ledger ("Brokeback Mountain"). Bob Dylan, John Fogerty and Eric Clapton also have sported the shirts.

In a 2004 Associated Press story on the company, blues and rock veteran Al Kooper said he had ordered shirts from Rockmount that week. "One of the biggest impressions on me is Elvis Presley. He wore Rockmount shirts," Kooper said.

Rockmount designed shirts for [the U.S. Congressional] delegation for the Democratic National Convention in Denver later this month.

The New York Times • August 14, 2008

Jack A. Weil, the Cowboy's Dresser, Dies at 107

By Douglas Martin

Jack A. Weil, a garter salesman, breezed into Denver in 1928 in a new Chrysler Roadster to start a new life. He exceeded his hopes and became a king of cowboy couture—almost certainly the first to put snaps on Western shirts (17 on a shirt), and most likely the first to produce bolo ties commercially.

• • •

Until Wednesday, when he died at 107 in Denver, Mr. Weil was still chief executive of the company he founded and, until just before his death, came to work daily. He was regularly called the oldest chief executive still working.

Known as Papa Jack, Mr. Weil said he owed his longevity to quitting smoking at 60 (after starting at 40), drinking at 90 and eating red meat at 100. He did have a medicinal shot of Jack Daniels twice a week.

The shirt—tailored close to the body, with "yokes" that seem to broaden the shoulders of cowpokes and city slickers alike and often with distinctive "smile" pockets—offers more than snaps. But snaps matter, not least to cowboys who are not handy at sewing. They break loose easily if the shirt is caught on a hostile horn. (They also offer a dramatic way to bare one's chest, but that might be another story.)

Western & English Today • September/October 2008
By Susan L. Ebert, Associate Publisher

As we go to press with this issue, the sad news of Jack A. Weil's passing has just crossed my desk.

At the age of 107, founder and CEO of Rockmount Ranch Wear—was the oldest working CEO in America.

The company he founded is credited with putting the "snap" in Western wear by creating the first Western shirts with snap fasteners, as well as the first commercially produced bolo ties.

• • •

The tapestry Jack built is the warp and woof of Western fashion as well as the spiritual fiber of The Cowboy Way itself. Adios, dear sir; *vaya con Dios*.

The Economist • August 28, 2008

Jack A. Weil, patriarch of western clothing, died on August 13th, aged 107

In the annals of fashion the snap-fastener, or press-stud, holds a humble place. Few care that it was invented in Germany, as the *Federknopf-Verschluss*, in the 1880s. Not many appreciate that some varieties have discs and grooves, while others boast sockets with studs. And almost no one considers that they give a man style. But Jack Weil did.

Mr. Weil reckoned that a cowboy on a horse, if wearing a shirt with buttons, was liable to get snagged on sagebrush or cactus or, worse than that, get a steerhorn straight through his fancy buttonhole. He was pretty certain, too, that a cowboy losing a button would feel disinclined to sew it on again. The answer to all those difficulties was to make shirts with snap-fasteners. And for 62 years, in a red-brick warehouse in the LoDo district of Denver, Mr. Weil did exactly that.

He also added a few more customisings. Pockets with sawtooth flaps, to keep tobacco in; a yoke fit, to broaden out the shoulders; body-hugging seams, to show the fine muscles of a cattleman; and deep cuffs. The hats, belts, buckles and bolo ties, which he also commercialized, were optional. But the snap-fasteners were *de rigueur*, topped with pearl and backed with tin, square or circular or diamond-shaped, strong enough to pass without cracking through the wringer of a 1940s washing-machine, and flash enough to turn heads on the streets of Denver on a Saturday night. "A cinch", as Mr. Weil proudly said.

Until he created his shirts, there was no distinctively western look in American couture. There were cowboys; but they wore dusty working clothes, accessorized with sweaty bandannas and clanking spurs, that no one much cared to copy. Indeed, Mr. Weil early on in his career made work-gear for cowboys, and learnt an important fact: they had no money. If he wanted to make any money himself, he would have to appeal not to the catwalk instincts of cattlemen, which were hard to spot, but to wannabe easterner cowboys who lived in, say, New York. Fortunately, there were plenty of them.